SIR
WILLIAM
WALLACE

GEDDES&GROSSET

This edition published 2000 by Geddes & Grosset, an imprint
of Children's Leisure Products Limited
Reprinted 2001

Adapted from a text by A. F. Murison

ISBN 1 85534 925 6

Printed and bound in Scotland

Contents

CHAPTER I

THE ENGLISH AGGRESSION

'Quhen Alysandyr oure Kyng wes dede,
   That Scotland led in luwe and lé,
Away wes sons of ale and brede,
   Off wyne and wax, off gamyn and glé:

'Oure gold wes changyd in to lede.
   Cryst, borne in to Vyrgynyté,
Succoure Scotland and remede,
   That stad [is in] perplexyté.'
                    Wyntoun, vii, *fin.*

A fateful date in the history of Scotland was 19 March 1286. At dusk that day, King Alexander III, riding along the coast of Fife near Kinghorn, was thrown over a precipice and killed. He was only forty-five years old, although in the thirty-seventh year of his reign. It is at this point in the history of Scotland that the contrast of peace and war is so apparent compared with any other moment in the annals of Scotland, or perhaps of any civilized nation in the world. This contrast forms an essential element in determining the judgment of history on the policy of the Scots and of the English kings.

At the death of Alexander, Scotland was a prosperous

country, steadily advancing in the arts of peaceful life – 'more civilized and more prosperous,' says Innes, with the common assent of historians, 'than at any period of her existence, down to the time when she ceased to be a separate kingdom in 1707.' The policy of Edward I, however motivated, was the prime cause of a lamentable subversion of the peace of a hundred years.

The Project of Marriage

The shadow of coming trouble had fallen on Scotland before the death of Alexander III. His family had been swept away by death. His first queen, Margaret, eldest daughter of Henry III and sister of Edward I of England, had died in 1275. His younger son, David, had died in 1280. His elder son, Alexander, who married Margaret, daughter of Guy, Count of Flanders, in 1282, had died without issue early in 1284. His only daughter, who married Eric II, king of Norway, in 1281, had also died early, in 1284, leaving a daughter. Alexander was still in his early forties, but there is no assurance of length of days and if he should die there would be a minority, probably a disputed succession, possibly an active revival of the English claim to overlordship.

In these circumstances, Alexander at once proceeded to take such precautions as he could. He summoned a parliament at Scone on 5 February 1284 and obtained from his nobles their solemn acknowledgment of Margaret, Princess of Norway, as heiress of Scotland in the event of his death. Towards the end of the next year, he married a second wife, Joleta (or Iolande), daughter of the Count de Dreux, but she bore him no child. Alexander must have often and anxiously reflected on the likelihood of a recurrence of the baronial rivalries that had proved a grave danger to the country during his own minority. On his tragic death on 19 March 1286, the hopes of the nation were left to rest on his granddaughter, the fragile Maid of Norway.

For a short period the affairs of the kingdom maintained a placid course. On 11 April 1286, the magnates assembled at Scone and selected six of their number to act as a Council of Regency with the official designation of 'the Guardians of the Kingdom of Scotland appointed by the common advice'. The Bishop of St Andrews and the Earls of Fife and Buchan were to administer the districts north of the Forth, the Bishop of Glasgow, Comyn of Badenoch and James the Steward of Scotland were to rule the lands south of the Forth. No question was raised as to the succession of the little princess and ostensibly there was every disposition on the part of the barons to fulfil the solemn pledges they had made to her grandfather two years before. It may, however, be open to doubt that an element of intrigue had developed by the time Alexander III was laid to rest at Dunfermline.

For one thing, there is in existence a letter of credence, dated Dunfermline, 29 March 1286, addressed to King Edward by the Bishops of St Andrews and Glasgow, 'in their own name, and in the name of the clergy, earls, barons, and all others of the realm of Scotland, who had been present at the burial of the lord Alexander of good memory, the late illustrious King of Scotland', and commending to Edward's confidence the two bearers, the prior of the Dominicans of Perth and Brother Arnold. The two friars were to deliver an oral communication and bring back the king's answer. There remains no record of the matter of either message or reply. It is difficult to believe that the business was merely a formal and complimentary communication. In view of the circumstances, it all but certainly must have borne reference, in part at least, to the settlement of the succession. The political record of the Bishop of St Andrews is not calculated to allay suspicion. Edward, at any rate, appears to have been satisfied, for he presently embarked for France and stayed away for more than three years.

Again, a few months later, Bruce of Annandale, ex-Chief Justice of England, smarting under his recent supersession, and his principal adherents took quiet action in view of contingencies. On 20 September, at his son's castle of Turnberry, fourteen Scots nobles – Patrick, Earl of Dunbar, and three sons, Walter, Earl of Menteith, and two sons, Bruce, lord of Annandale, and two sons, James, Steward (and one of the Guardians) of Scotland, John, his brother, and Angus, son of Donald of the Isles, and his son – entered into a stringent bond obliging them to give faithful adherence to Richard de Burgh, Earl of Ulster, and Lord Thomas de Clare (brother of Gilbert, Earl of Gloucester, Edward's son-in-law and Bruce's brother-in-law) 'in their affairs'. The nature of these affairs is not indicated; neither is there any other record of them. There is a suggestive clause pledging their fealty to the king of England and to 'him that shall obtain the kingdom of Scotland through blood relationship with King Alexander of blessed memory, according to the ancient customs in the Kingdom of Scotland approved and observed.' There is no direct reference to the child queen.

It is useless to inquire what the business was that Richard de Burgh and Thomas de Clare had in hand or in contemplation. Plainly the instrument was simply a diplomatic process of binding all the parties together in support of such action as Bruce might take on the advice of a majority of their number for advancing his pretensions to the throne of Scotland when opportunity should serve. There is nothing to show that Edward ever had knowledge of this bond.

Somewhere about this time, moreover, Bruce passed from speculation to action. Balliol, in his pleadings before Edward in 1291, averred that, in violation of their oath of fealty to Queen Margaret, 'Sir Robert Bruce and the Earl of Carrick, his son, attacked the castle of Dumfries with fire and arms, and banners displayed, and against the peace expelled the forces of the Queen, who held the same. Hence Sir Robert advanced to the castle of Buittle. He then caused a proclamation to be made by one Patrick M'Guffock, within the bailiary of the said castle,' with the result that good subjects were driven from the land. 'Furthermore,' the allegation ran, 'the Earl of Carrick, by the assent and power of his father, took the Lady of Scotland's castle of Wigton, and killed several of her people there.' A number of entries in the Exchequer Rolls combine to support Balliol's charge and even to show that the wave of disturbance was felt on the eastern seaboard. How Bruce was brought back to peaceable ways does not appear.

The temporary stir occasioned by Bruce's eagerness was the only ripple on the face of affairs for some three years. Early in 1289, however, Edward seems to have made up his mind to strengthen his hold on Scotland by a marriage between the young queen and Prince Edward of Wales. The proposed parties, being cousins-german, were within the degrees prohibited by canon law, and on 8 May Edward dispatched Sir Otho de Grandison to Rome with letters from himself and a petition from the prince, soliciting from Pope

Nicholas IV the necessary dispensation. The idea may have presented itself to Edward's mind two years earlier, for on 27 May 1287 he had obtained a bull from Pope Honorius IV permitting him to marry his children to relatives in the fourth degree of affinity or consanguinity. However this may be, in April and May 1289 envoys passed to and fro between Edward and Eric on 'certain affairs', which were no doubt affairs tending in the direction of the marriage.

On 6 November commissioners representing the three countries concerned met at Salisbury and concluded a treaty. Eric was to send the queen to England or to Scotland by 1 November the next year, free from matrimonial engagement. If she came to England, Edward would, on the establishment of security and peace in Scotland, and on the demand of the Scots nation, send her to Scotland, again free from matrimonial engagement, provided 'the good nation of Scotland' gave 'sufficient and good security' to Edward not to marry her without the appointment and advice of himself and the assent of the king of Norway. The Scots envoys engaged to establish such order as to allow the queen quiet enjoyment of her realm. The preamble of the treaty is framed so as to convey that Eric was the prime mover in the business. He is represented as having applied to Edward for aid and advice, the object being to secure for Edward's niece the obedience of her subjects and the free exercise and enjoyment of her royal powers after the manner of other kings in their own kingdoms.

On receiving this appeal, Edward, in his zeal for the peace of Scotland and for the establishment of his niece in her rightful position, invited the Guardians to send commissioners to the Salisbury convention. But there can be no doubt that Edward himself was the prime mover. Eric certainly was loth to part with his child; he had made no representation on her behalf to the Scots Guardians, nor had they indicated any wish to have her in Scotland. On the other hand, Edward's project of marriage would naturally require her presence on this side of the North Sea, and his influence with Eric was backed by a recent loan of 2000 marks, with easy arrangements for repayment, which seems not to have been yet discharged.

It may be doubted whether Edward was taking all this trouble out of disinterested anxiety for the welfare and royal status of his niece or for the security of peace on the English border. The treaty gives no hint that the Salisbury commissioners had before them the marriage contemplated by Edward. The terms of the engagement of the Scots, as well as the absence of an express statement, would seem to negate the idea. Sufficient reason may be found in the fact that the papal dispensation had not then been granted as well as in Edward's desire to proceed cautiously. It is to be noted that not only in the treaty but also in the prince's petition to the pope and in a communication of Edward's addressed to the Scottish people on the same day as the treaty was made, and counselling the obedience of all to the Guardians, the great object of the peace and reformation of Scotland is dwelt on with suspicious emphasis. Sir Otho de Grandison returned to London on 31 December. With the irony of fate, the dispensation, which had been granted (and acknowledged handsomely in gold florins) on 16 November, did not arrive in the form of a papal bull until 9 October 1290, almost simultaneously with the arrival of the rumour of the queen's death.

At a conference held at Brigham on 14 March 1290, the treaty of Salisbury was confirmed. Three days later, the Guardians, who had now at least been informed of Edward's intention and of the dispensation, addressed a letter to Edward assenting to the proposed marriage and another letter to Eric urging him to send Margaret at once to England. It may seem strange that they should not have asked him to send her to Scotland, but Edward obviously had laid great stress on the alleged risks of the unsettled condition of the country. His solicitude, from a family point of view, was not at all unreasonable, and probably he had impressed Eric with anxiety on the same ground; and the Guardians seem to have had no serious anticipation that their queen's grand-uncle would infringe the international friendship of a century. The Guardians' letter to Eric was followed by one from Edward on the same subject on 17 April.

Already the king's butler was down at Yarmouth, preparing and provisioning 'a great ship' to carry Edward's envoy, Antony Bek, the astute and magnificent Bishop of Durham, with an imposing retinue, to Norway. The preparations took forty days and Bek sailed from Hartlepool on 9 May. Bek was an adept in smoothing the diplomatic path. He distributed judicious annuities to Norwegian friends to the extent of £400 a year until the queen should attain the age of fifteen. Presumably the grand outfitting of the ship implies that the queen was expected to come over in it, but it returned without her in June. It was not until September that Eric set out with his daughter.

Edward again dispatched Bek, this time to Orkney, to meet the Maid. He was also attentive enough to send an ample variety of jewels for the queen's use. At almost every step in the proceedings, the records betray his eager haste. The Guardians exhibited no such fervour. It was not until 3 October that they accredited their envoys and already they had been urged to action by Edward.

Meantime the Guardians had been taking thought for the security of the kingdom. The negotiations with Edward were issued in the treaty of Brigham on 18 July 1290. By this treaty it was provided that the laws, liberties and customs of Scotland should remain inviolate for ever and that the realm should remain separate from, and entirely independent of, England. No parchment terms could have done more to secure independence. There was, however, an insidious saving clause steadily recurrent that reserved such rights as Edward or others might have, but whether intended to neutralize the specific provisions or not, it must be regarded as purely formal.

The ardent development of Edward's care for his grandniece and his son ought to have been at least suggestive. There remain two striking documents dated 28 August. In one, the Guardians agree to deliver the castles of Scotland under certain conditions to their queen and Prince Edward, and in the other Edward notifies the Guardians of his appointment of Bishop Bek to act in concert with them as lieutenant of the royal couple, for it was incumbent on him to respect his oath to maintain the laws of Scotland. He even appears to have gone so far as to demand the surrender of the castles to himself, but this demand the Guardians refused.

The whole of the laborious structure was levelled to the ground on 7 October when the Bishop of St Andrews reported to Edward the rumour of the queen's death at Orkney. The queen had died on the passage from 'Norrowa' o'er the faem'. The details are unknown. The very fact, indeed, has been questioned, for a young woman claiming to be Margaret and telling a circumstantial story of her being kidnapped at Orkney on the voyage to Scotland, was burnt at the stake at Bergen in 1301 as an impostor. Be this as it may, the luckless Margaret now passes out of the history of Scotland, leaving a divided kingdom face to face with the aroused cupidity of a determined, astute and unscrupulous neighbour.

The Assertion of Overlordship

Who should now succeed Margaret on the Scottish throne? Fordun relates that Malcolm, the first 'rex Scotiae', decreed a change in the principle of succession. This enactment is said to have provided that henceforward each king should be succeeded by whoever was, at the time, the next descendant; that is, a son or a daughter, a nephew or a niece, the nearest then living.

It is likely that the disturbance of the balance of the kingdom by the acquisition of Lothian may have rendered the substitution of the Teutonic for the Celtic law of succession expedient or even necessary. The claims of Balliol and Bruce alone need to be considered, and if this law was formally established, the letter of it would be a strong support to Bruce's candidature, whatever the spirit of its intention. For the present purpose, however, we are not concerned with the validity of the claims of either competitor but mainly with the process whereby the final decision was reached. The essential point is to discern the real spirit governing the evolution of events.

The death of Margaret at once urged the competitors to

fresh activity. The Guardians were divided in their sympathies, and the division no doubt ran deep into the community. The first overt movement, as far as existing documents indicate, was made by Bruce. It was an indirect, tentative operation. Towards the end of the year (1290), an appeal was preferred to Edward by 'the seven earls' and the community of the realm of Scotland against the Bishop of St Andrews and Sir John Comyn in respect of their action as Guardians. The appellants asserted their privilege of placing the king of Scotland on the throne, complained of acts of oppression exercised by the Guardians on Donald, Earl of Mar, and the freemen of Moray, narrated the recognition of Robert Bruce of Annandale as next heir to the throne by Alexander II, and alleged some minor grievances. At this time there were only four Guardians, the Earl of Fife having been murdered and the Earl of Buchan having died, and the two not inculpated, the Steward of Scotland and the Bishop of Glasgow, were friends of Bruce. Mar and Moray also leant towards Bruce. Evidently the appeal was promoted in the interests of Bruce and with his knowledge if not positively at his instigation. There is no record of any answer.

There is a glimpse of still earlier action by Bruce in the letter of the Bishop of St Andrews to Edward reporting the rumour of the queen's death. The rumour arrived when the Estates were sitting to receive Edward's answer to the refusal to surrender the castles to him. Bruce, the Bishop says, had not intended to be present but, on hearing the rumour, had appeared with a strong following. His ultimate intentions the bishop could not tell. Then follows a significant point. Should it unhappily prove true that the queen is dead, the bishop urges Edward to come to the marches without delay with the view of preventing bloodshed and of aiding the faithful of the land to place on the throne the man who possesses the proper title – meaning, of course, Balliol. To interpret the bishop as merely currying favour with the king is probably a large stretch of charity. He certainly stood in a small minority in desiring Edward's intervention. The chroniclers, indeed, relate how the community of the realm, impressed by the ancient friendship between the two kingdoms and the particular cordiality of Alexander III and Edward, invited the English king to arbitrate on the claims of the competitors. But no such invitation is traceable in the records, and, on that ground alone, apart from the strong probabilities, it may safely be believed that such an invitation was never sent. There was not the least occasion for it on either side. It certainly would not have represented the true feeling of the community of Scotland and no doubt Edward was fully aware of the fact, for, in the whole transaction, he studiously treated that body with scant regard.

The Waverley Annalist states that in March 1291, on the day after Ascension, Edward declared to his nobles in the presence of nine of the competitors, who at the same time submitted their claims to him, that he was resolved to subdue Scotland as he had recently subdued Wales. But Edward was now on the peaceful tack of legal process. The competitors, although mostly Scots nobles, were also mostly the liegemen of Edward for large possessions in England, and not one of them could dare to claim the throne of Scotland without regard to Edward's opinion. It was quite inevitable that every one of them should submit to his judgment. Besides their material interests in England, they were of Norman descent and upbringing and had Norman sympathies, and thus they were largely alien to the mass of the Scottish population. Their interest in Scotland was little, if anything, more than a matter of land and lordship. They were quite content to take the kingdom of Scotland as a bigger fief. It was therefore the most natural thing in the world for them to leave the decision of the case in the hands of their liege lord, the king of England. For the community of Scotland the question wore a wholly different aspect.

Edward had taken good care not to allow the matter to rest through the winter. He had sent orders to all the religious houses in the land requiring them to search diligently in their chronicles and to transmit to him speedily extracts of all such passages as might bear on the relations of England and Scotland. Such of these extracts as had come to hand he caused to be read out to his parliament assembled at Norham on 10 May. Through his Justiciary, Sir Roger le Brabazon, he set forth his solicitude for the peace of Scotland and his anxiety to do justice to all, and required the Scots prelates and nobles to recognize his superiority and direct lordship – a claim affirmed to be 'clear, from chronicles found in different monasteries and other places in England and Scotland, from other sources of information, from certain documents, and on most evident reasons.' The Scots nobles present, although previously informed of Edward's intentions, represented their inability to reply without further consultation with nobles and others not then present. The meeting was adjourned until the next day when Bishop Bek, not Edward personally, announced that they might take three weeks, at the end of which time they would be expected to produce any evidence they might be able to find against the king's claim of superiority.

Meanwhile, the returns from the religious houses continued to pour in. The Scots nobles also must have shown anxiety for the independence of Scotland, for on 31 May Edward made them a declaration that the coming of the magnates and the Community of Scotland to Norham should not be drawn into a precedent in prejudice of the liberties of the realm. Then, on 2 June, the Scots nobles assembled on Upsetlington Green – Holywell Haugh – on the north side of the Tweed opposite Norham Castle. The Bishop of Bath and Wells, Chancellor of England, with the usual preliminary flourish about the gracious feelings and intentions of Edward, informed them that the kings of England from the remotest times had held the overlordship of Scotland. They themselves, he pointed out, had not even now brought forward any evidence to disprove Edward's claim. Edward, therefore, in the exercise of his right, would proceed to investigate and decide the rights of the claimants. Eight of these who were present formally acknowledged Edward's supremacy.

Next day the proceedings were resumed on the English side of the Tweed in the parish church of Norham. Balliol, who had been absent on the previous day, now made his acknowledgment. The Bishop of Bath and Wells advanced Edward's pretensions another step. He explained that Edward did not construe the possession and exercise of his right of overlordship as excluding his hereditary right of lordship. Then, as to the way of determining among the claims of the competitors, Edward suggested that the chief claimants, Balliol and Bruce, should each, on behalf of themselves and such other competitors as should agree, nominate forty arbiters or auditors, the king himself being content to nominate twenty-four, more or less, to hear the evidence and to report to him, whereupon he would give his decision. The hundred and four arbiters were appointed accordingly on 5 July, and the next day they fixed the hearing to take place at Berwick, the king himself appointing 2 August as the date.

The 11th of June had been a memorable day. The Guardians formally resigned the kingdom and its castles to Edward as overlord. The Bishop of Caithness, on the nomination of the Scots nobles, was appointed by Edward Chancellor of Scotland; and with him was associated the king's own clerk, Sir Walter de Amundesham (Amersham), who was presently (18 August) succeeded by Adam de Botingdon. Two days later Sir Brian Fitz Alan was associated with the Guardians in Edward's interest; the first batch of Scots prelates and barons swore fealty on the Holy Evangels, and Edward, 'as overlord of Scotland', ordered the governors of castles in Scotland to deliver them over to governors of his own appointment, the common consent of the Scots Guardians and of the competitors being recorded, and Edward as overlord proclaimed his peace.

On 17 June a general order was issued that all freeholders should swear fealty to Edward. The terms of the ordinance as to homage and fealty, which had been settled on 12 June at Norham by Edward 'with the advice of the prelates and magnates of Scotland there present', were comprehensive and precise. They applied to 'all, both clerical and lay, who would have been bound to make homage and fealty to a living king of Scotland.' All who came were to be admitted. Those who came and refused were to be arrested until performance. Those who did not come but excused themselves for good reason were to be allowed until the next parlia-

ment. Those who neither came nor excused themselves
were to be 'more straitly distrained' until they conformed.
Thus, to all appearances, Edward held Scotland in the grip
of his iron hand – the reward of a patient diplomacy.

The great process was resumed on 3 August at Berwick.
The competitors, now increased to twelve, presented their
claims in technical form before the hundred and four auditors. The first object was to decide the point of law at issue
between Balliol and Bruce, namely, whether the nearer descendant by the younger child or the more remote descendant by the elder child had the preferable title. 'Perhaps,' as
Burton says, 'the policy of the arrangement lay in this, that
in Bruce and Balliol, and those they might bring with them,
the Lord Superior knew whom he had to deal with personally; among a set of miscellaneous strangers, bringing their
friends and supporters into the controversy, he might find
troublesome people.' The question, if in some sense 'a by-
question between two claimants', nevertheless went to the
root of the claims of the two competitors that were obviously first in the running. The proceedings went on without
getting much farther forward until 12 August, when Edward
adjourned the sittings to 2 June 1292.

It had been alleged that a document on which was
founded the claim of the Count of Holland was missing, and
this gave the king a welcome opportunity of further demonstrating his resolution to do justice to the last iota. On this
12 August he appointed certain commissioners to examine
all documents presented by suitors or 'in any way touching
us and our kingdom', whether in Edinburgh Castle or elsewhere in Scotland. Under the order many papers were carried away and deposited in Berwick Castle. It does not ap-

pear that anything of importance or of immediate relevance was discovered. Certainly Edward found nothing to support his claim of overlordship, otherwise he would have utilized it and had it carefully recorded. Whatever his real intention in directing the search, his subsequent dealings with Scotland gave colour – and probably quite false colour – to later allegations charging him with the express purpose of wantonly destroying the national records. During the next five or six days (13–18 August), Edward manifested his satisfaction with events in a manner peculiarly pleasing to some half-dozen Scots magnates. There remains a record of certain grants he made to the Bishop of Glasgow, James, Steward of Scotland, Earl Patrick of Dunbar, Sir John de Soulis, Sir William de St Clair, Sir Patrick de Graham and Sir William de Soulis. These grants are expressed to be made for various expenditure and 'also for the zeal' the grantee 'had and has to promote peace and tranquillity among the people' of Scotland. The record, however, is cancelled in the Rolls for the very sufficient reason that the particular grants were not made after all, equivalents being given instead.

While English counsels ruled the policy of the Guardians and English castellans stretched their mailed hands over Scotland from the strongholds, the great cause dragged on. At length, 2 June 1292 came round and Edward resumed the process at Berwick. A thirteenth competitor now presented himself – Eric, king of Norway. Edward professed anxiety to reach a decision, for was he not moved by the sore desolation of Scotland? Still the contest surged about the claims of Bruce and Balliol. How to arrive at the right decision? The Scots auditors would greatly assist the king to expedite matters if they would inform him on what laws and customs he is to proceed. The Scots auditors are helpless to decide without further consideration and advice; perhaps the English auditors would aid them? The English auditors join in consultation, but they shrink from answering without further and more precise advice which they might perhaps obtain from the prelates and nobles of England. Apparently then, there must be a further adjournment. Edward accordingly fixed 14 October for the next meeting and stated that in the meantime he and the rest of the parties interested would take the best advice to be found anywhere in the two kingdoms.

It is not relevant to pursue the arguments of the October meeting. On the 15th the case was closed, no doubt after private diplomatic dealing with the competitors. On 17 November, Edward announced his decision in great state in the hall of Berwick Castle – in favour of Balliol. Thereupon he issued orders to the Guardians to deliver seisin of the kingdom to the new king and to the castellans of the twenty-three chief strongholds to deliver them over to Balliol or his representatives. On the 20th, Balliol swore fealty to Edward at Norham; on the 30th he was enthroned at Scone; then he went back to Newcastle-upon-Tyne and, having eaten his Christmas dinner with his overlord, did homage to him next morning as an invested king.

On 2 January, by letters patent sealed by Balliol, by two great prelates and by ten of the principal nobles of Scotland, Edward was acquitted of all obligations incurred by him while the country was in his hands, and two days later he acknowledged that his rights in Scotland were limited to homage and its pertinents. Some special favours of a financial nature within the next few months intimate Edward's satisfaction with his royal henchman. But these marks of the overlord's pleasure were far from counterbalancing the dissatisfaction openly and ominously manifested in the kingdom of Scotland.

Two or three points in this prolonged process invite particular remark. In the first place, as Burton justly points out,

'What confers a strange interest on the selfish squabble and the array of technicalities and pleadings called out by it, is that there is no more allusion to the rights of the Community of Scotland, or the way in which a decision may affect them, than there need be in any private litigation. They have no more place in the question than the tenants on an estate while the settlements are disputed. So far as one can gather from the terms of the documents, it never seems to have occurred to the greedy litigants themselves or their astute technical advisers, that there was a fierce self-willed people, nourished in independence and national pride, who must be bent or broken before the subtleties and pedantries of the Lord Superior's court would be of any avail. Totally unconscious they seem also to have been that the intricate technicalities which dealt with a sovereign independent State as a mere piece of property in search of an owner, formed an insult never to be forgiven, whatever might be the cost of repudiation and vengeance.'

Edward himself, however, was gifted with a deeper insight than all the rest. He at least was thoroughly aware of the deeper elements of the problem and of their difficult character. At the Upsetlington meeting, while the prelates and nobles had nothing to urge against Edward's claims – for Wyntoun's record of the Bishop of Glasgow's bold denial of the pretended right of superiority must be held in suspense

– the 'Community' of Scotland undoubtedly presented a protest. What this body had to say on the point most unfortunately we do not know. It finds no place in the very full record of proceedings preserved in the Great Roll of Scotland. There is, however, no doubt at all that some answer was made and that it was set aside as 'nothing to the point' (*nihil efficax*). But Burton's comment deserves to be carefully borne in mind. 'Transactions,' he shrewdly remarks, 'are profusely recorded, as if for the purpose of courting all inquiry into doubts or difficulties that might affect conclusions, yet one ever feels, throughout all this candour, that the truth is to be found somewhere behind, and that the abundance of punctilious record is devised to conceal it.' The exclusion of all notice of the action of the Community from the official record must be taken to have been deliberate. But it was an act of policy, not of inappreciation, on the part of the king.

There is another element in certain documents of the time that confirms this conclusion in a striking manner. In the official record of the case, Edward is designated Lord Superior at every turn. There is a marked contrast, however, in the order he directed to each of the Scots castellans to deliver over their strongholds to English successors. 'In the preamble,' Burton points out, 'Edward does not make display of his office of Lord Superior, as in the documents which were not to go to Scotland. He is Edward, King of England, Lord of Ireland, and Duke of Guienne; and he demands delivery of the fortress by assent of the Guardians and of the several candidates, and only towards the conclusion does he briefly bring in his title of "Soveryn Seygnur".' In this order, as well as in the order as to fealty, he judiciously associates with himself the prelates and magnates of the realm of Scotland. Obviously he exercised sleepless discretion in the pushing of his claims, with a careful eye on the possible effects in a high-spirited community.

A word may also be said on the functions of the auditors. From the record of their appointment, it would seem to be plain enough that they were intended to sit together as a single board of referees. The magnanimity of Edward and his confidence in the justice of his cause were not ignored by the English chroniclers; eighty to twenty-four manifests a generosity of fairness. But then we have already seen that the auditors did not, at any rate always, act as a single body. At a late stage of the proceedings, two questions arose: by what law should the question be tried – by the Imperial (that is, the Civil or Roman) law or by the laws and customs of England or Scotland? Is there any specialty in rank or dignity of this kingdom of Scotland that should exempt it from being adjudicated upon like the other tenures of the realm? 'On these two questions,' says Burton, 'King Edward's own council of twenty-four were alone consulted. "Those of Scotland", as the persons selected by Bruce and Balliol were termed, had no opportunity of recording their opinion on these, which, of all the questions put, were the most eminently national in their character.' This is a somewhat startling result in view of the expectations raised by the terms of appointment. 'Yet,' Burton proceeds, 'it was so managed that they too should appear to have had a voice. It was put to the claimants, Balliol and Bruce, and to the eighty of Scotland selected by them, whether they could show any cause why the kingdom of Scotland – a fief of the king of England – should be treated differently from earldoms, baronies and other tenures. Under nice distinctions in the ways of putting questions, the broad fact can be distinctly traced that the twenty-four of England were advisers or referees of the supreme judge, Edward himself, as to the judgment to be given, while the eighty of Scotland were merely the advisers of the two claimants as to the position they should take up as litigants – what they should admit, and what they should dispute. Accordingly, the eighty are not heard in answer to the questions put; the competitors, Balliol and Bruce, give the answers.' Even, however, if the apparent intention to constitute a single board of one hundred and four had been consistently maintained, the result would have been practically the same. The Balliol and the Bruce men would have neutralized each other and the English twenty-four would have decided every point – and that, too, inevitably in the sense conformable to the mind of the king of England. The whole process was a gigantic palaver, impressing the grandeur, the legality and the considerateness of Edward while utilized as a cloak and a means for the remorseless prosecution of his designs upon the independence of Scotland.

It remains to inquire briefly into the substantial validity of the claim of overlordship. It might augur industrious adventure to penetrate to the misty age of Brute the Trojan and Scota, the daughter of the king of Egypt. It would be little less futile to trace the records of the chronicles collected by Edward from the time of Edward the Elder down through four centuries. It is hardly worthwhile even to deal with the submission of William the Lion when he was accidentally captured in 1174 before Alnwick Castle on a raid into the north of England. The facts have been obscured by the greater anxiety of historians to fit them in with their preconceptions than to ascertain precisely the meaning of the plain record. If the release of William's obligations by Richard for 10,000 marks to eke out his preparations for a crusade has any meaning at all, it means clearly the restoration of the absolute independence of Scotland. The treaty of Falaise 'created the new condition of vassal and superior from that date'; and the Canterbury transactions released William from all the engagements that Henry II thereby 'extorted from him,' as Richard's charter phrases it, 'by new deeds and by consequence of his captivity.' The competitor who submitted to Edward that Richard could not legally release the homage of Scotland was either praiseworthily exhaustive or hopelessly barren of argument. It seems to demand a facile credulity to believe that William gave 10,000 marks to be released from one ground of an obligation that still remained valid against him on another ground not even specified in express terms, or that Richard placidly went off to the crusade leaving on the northern marches of England an inviting opportunity to an active and aggrieved neighbour. That William should do homage for his estates in England was a matter of course but quite a different matter.

Henry III appears indeed to have entertained the claim of overlordship. There is no reference to homage, however, in connection with the treaty of Newcastle. Henry and Alexander II simply engaged not to abet each other's enemies and not to invade other's territories without just provocation. Nor, when Alexander III succeeded to the throne in 1249 at the age of seven, did Henry put forward any claim of wardship – a fact especially significant of the relations between the kingdoms. It is no doubt true that Henry prayed Pope Innocent IV to prohibit the anointing and crowning of the child king of Scots on the ground that Alexander was his liege vassal, for so much appears from the pope's letter of refusal dated 1251. But Henry does not seem to have proceeded further in the matter. It is stated that on the occasion of Alexander's marriage with his daughter Margaret in 1252 at York, Henry demanded homage for Scotland as a fief of England and that the reply of the boy king that he could not take such an important step without the knowledge and assent of his parliament, closed the question. The reply bears evident witness to the vigilance of Alexander's advisers. The same vigilance is to be seen in the terms of the safe-conduct of Alexander and his queen to England in 1260. Neither the king nor his attendants should be required to deal with state affairs during the visit. In fact, Henry III, whatever his theoretical claims, never exercised the right of overlordship. On the contrary, whenever he did interfere in the affairs of Alexander's kingdom, it was in the capacity of a friendly father-in-law and under the style of 'Principal Councillor to the illustrious King of Scotland'.

The case of 1278 is strikingly illustrative. In that year, Alexander did homage to Edward I at Westminster, and the fact is recorded in a transcript of a Close Roll in absolute terms: 'I, Alexander, King of the Scots, become liege man of the Lord Edward, King of the English, against all nations.' Allen verified the entry and found that the writing was on an erasure. The suspicion aroused by the erasure is not lightened by the record of the proceedings preserved in the register of Dunfermline Abbey. There the scribe expressed the homage of Alexander very differently: 'I become your man for the lands which I hold of you in the kingdom of England, for which I owe you homage, saving my kingdom.' Furthermore, it is added: 'Then said the Bishop of Norwich,

"And saving to the King of England, if he right have, your homage for your kingdom," to whom the King instantly replied, saying openly, "To homage for my kingdom of Scotland no man has right, except God alone, nor do I hold that kingdom otherwise than of God alone.'" The vague and insidious use of such expressions as 'if he right have', 'whatever right he may have' or 'whenever he chooses to exercise his right' fostered the tendency to elevate a claim into a right. It indicates that there actually existed no right capable of definite formulation on firm grounds or at any rate no right capable of assertion. The gross falsification of such records permits us to hold the Dunfermline scribe as at least an equal authority with the Westminster scribe. This convenient vagueness of suggestion of right reappears with like tameness in the tail of the treaty of Brigham.

Did King Edward honestly believe that he was entitled to the homage of the new king of Scots? The question may be least ungraciously answered by another question: Suppose the sides reversed, would Edward have submitted with intellectual conviction to the same claim advanced against himself on the same grounds? It would be to libel his intelligence. It is impossible to believe that he cared one atom for the chronicles he marshalled so industriously except for indirect purposes. It is easy enough to understand that his conception of policy could readily justify a wrong as ministerial to what he conceived to be a higher right.

The Triumph of Aggression

Uneasy lay the head that wore the crown of Scotland. The flatteries of King John's friends could not blind him to his isolation. The formal respect rendered to him often betrayed

33

not merely reluctance but defiance and contempt. The leading men of the dissident factions soon proceeded to remove
his friends from his side and to surround him with strangers
and even to take out of his control the direction of affairs.
The St Albans Annalist records that John dared not open his
mouth in case his people in their rage should starve him or
throw him into a dungeon; 'he was like a lamb in the midst
of wolves.'

John's uneasiness was not mitigated by the action of his
feudal lord. Edward mixed his early desires to please with
disagreeable reminders. On 31 December 1292 he required
John to attend at Newcastle the appeal of Roger Bartholo-
mew, a burgess of Berwick. In vain, John pointed Edward to
the convention of Brigham under which no Scotsman was
to be required to plead in any legal proceeding outside the
realm of Scotland. Edward insisted on the cancellation not
only of the convention but of every document, known or
unknown, calculated to restrict in any way the free exercise
of his superiority.

Again, on 8 March, John was cited to answer in the English court for denial of justice to the indefatigable John
Mazun, a merchant of Gascony, who had a big claim against
the late Alexander III. In a fortnight's time, 25 March, John
was again cited to appear before the English parliament to
answer an appeal of Macduff of Kilconquhar from a decision
of the Scots parliament in February. John did not appear.

He was again cited to appear on 14 October. He did appear then, but the only answer to be extracted from him was
that he dare not act without consultation with the Estates of
his realm – an answer probably put in his mouth by his Stirling parliament in August. He was imposed with heavy dam-

ages, and on the principle that the wrongdoer should be punished, it was resolved that the three principal castles in Scotland with their towns should be delivered over to the Lord Superior until he ceased his obstinate resistance. John humbled himself, however, before judgment was formally given and Edward granted a further postponement. Meanwhile, in June and September, two more summonses had come and two more followed in November. The English parliament had, indeed, passed certain standing orders including one that tolerated no excuse of absence from either party. John was bound to be constantly trotting up and down on the most trivial matters. Edward was undoubtedly within his technical rights, and as Lord Hailes says, he was bent on exercising them 'with the most provoking rigour'. 'It is easy to see,' as Burton remarks, 'that his immediate object was to subject his new vassal to deep humiliation.'

Meantime the king of France was preparing to deal out to Edward the same measure as Edward was meting out to John. He summoned Edward to answer before the Twelve Peers in December for certain acts of aggression of Englishmen upon French subjects in the preceding spring. Regarding the summons as a pretext for the annexation of his French dominions, Edward stayed at home and played for time. But in February Philip declared him to be opposing lawful authority with contempt and in May pronounced forfeiture of his lands. Edward kept up negotiations but prepared for war, and as overlord of Scotland, he summoned Balliol and twenty-one Scots magnates to join him with their forces at London on 1 September 1294. John attended the English parliament and contributed three years' rental for his large English estates, but his magnates disregarded the summons and, when pressed, declared a lack of sufficient means.

Edward's difficulties between France and Wales as well as at home gave both encouragement and opportunity to the discontent that was seething in Scotland. A parliament was held at Scone. The Estates dismissed all English court officials and appointed a Council of Twelve, probably after the model of the Twelve Peers of the king of France, to conduct the government. John was formally reduced to a figurehead. Urged by his Council and stung by the humiliations heaped upon him by Edward, he entered into a secret alliance, offensive and defensive, with Philip of France under which his son and heir, Edward Balliol, was to marry Philip's niece, the eldest daughter of Charles, Count of Valois and Anjou. John accredited his envoys to Philip in July 1295, the treaty was signed by Philip in October and John ratified it at Dunfermline on 23 February 1296 with the assent not only of his prelates and nobles but also of the chief burgh corporations and other public bodies of the kingdom. The scheme was carefully placed 'on a broad popular basis', and it seems to have been arranged with as little publicity as was consistent with a wide representation of the nation. 'This was the starting of that great policy which had so much influence for centuries on both sides of the British Channel – the policy of France and Scotland taking common counsel against England.'

In the course of the early autumn of 1295, it is likely that Edward got wind of John's treasonable activities. He issued summonses for his memorable parliament of November. Perhaps as a feeler, he required John to expel all Frenchmen and Flemings, his enemies, from Scotland or to put in his

hands the three castles and towns of the eastern frontier –
Berwick, Roxburgh and Jedburgh. The first alternative was
firmly refused, but it appears from an existing document
that the castles were delivered over to the Bishop of Carlisle.

On 16 October there are two remarkable records: one is
the engagement of Edward to his 'beloved and faithful' John
to redeliver the three castles and towns at the end of the
French war; the other is a circular order to all the sheriffs in
England to take into the king's hand all the lands and goods
of Balliol and of all other Scotsmen staying in Scotland
within their respective jurisdictions. Were these castles ever
delivered to Edward? Was the engagement of 16 October
(with the order to the bishop to take delivery, dated 12 October) only anticipatory and never operative? There is, indeed,
strong historical support to the view that the Scots absolutely refused both alternatives and shook in Edward's face
Pope Celestine's absolution of them from homage and fealty.
The confiscation order was probably Edward's counterstroke.
It was followed up on 13 February by an order for the sale of
all goods on such lands excepting only agricultural stock and
implements, the proceeds to go into the Exchequer.

The inevitable collision was precipitated by an incident at
Berwick in which some English merchants were killed and
their goods seized. On 23 February, Edward issued urgent
orders to speed up the forces appointed to meet him at
Newcastle-upon-Tyne, directing that 'neither for assizes,
gaol deliveries, or any other business' is the Sheriff of York to
hinder the men of his county from arriving on the appointed day, apparently 1 March. He summoned John to
Newcastle to answer for the Berwick riot and his breaches
of allegiance, but of course John declined the invitation.

About the middle of March, Edward moved to Wark, just abandoned by the romantically traitorous Robert de Ros, but he appears to have had scruples about beginning the invasion of Scotland until Easter was past. Then, on 28 March, he passed the Tweed with 30,000 foot soldiers and 5000 armed horsemen, and on 30 March he took Berwick town without any effective opposition. As Burton records:

> 'There is an awful unanimity of testimony to the merciless use made of the victory. The writer who knew best of all describes the king as rabid, like a boar infested with the hounds, and issuing the order to spare none; and tells how the citizens fell like the leaves in autumn, until there was not one of the Scots who could not escape left alive, and he rejoices over their fate as a just judgment for their wickedness.'

The gallantry of the Flemings in defence of their Red Hall only ensured their destruction. 'Thus it was on the community among whom the protection of the Lord Superior was first sought that his vengeance first fell.' Berwick, 'the great city of merchant princes', a 'second Alexandria', was reduced to a common market town. 'Such a massacre,' says Pearson, 'had not been witnessed within the four seas since the ravage of the North by the Conqueror. From this time a sea of blood lay between the English king and his Scottish dominion.' The castle was surrendered the same day by Sir William Douglas, on guarantee of the lives of the garrison. Edward remained at Berwick nearly a month, actively re-fortifying the town.

In Berwick Castle, on 5 April, Edward received John's formal renunciation. John bluntly complained that he had been wrongly cited to England at the trifling instance of anybody and everybody; and through no fault of his, Edward had taken possession of his and his subjects' castles, lands and possessions within his kingdom of Scotland; that Edward had taken his and his subjects' goods by land and sea and transferred them to England; that Edward had killed merchants and other inhabitants of his kingdom; that Edward had forcibly carried off subjects of his from Scotland and detained them in prison in England; that Edward had paid no heed to his representations; and that Edward had publicly summoned his army and had now come with 'an innumerable multitude of armed men' to strip him and his subjects of their inheritance, and had approached with hostile intent the boundaries of his kingdom and had crossed them and had committed atrocities of slaughter, arson and violence by land and sea. John therefore resigned his obligations and homage on behalf of himself and all others of his realm who might adhere to him.

'Has the felon fool done such a silly thing?' the king is said to have exclaimed. 'If he will not come to us, we will go to him.'

But it is far from apparent why Edward should have manifested any such surprise.

On 26 March, while Edward was at Wark, a large body of Scots under Comyn, Earl of Buchan, made a foray from Annandale into Cumberland, assaulting Carlisle (where Bruce of Annandale was governor) and burning a large part of the city. On 8 April, too, a foray was made by the same body from Jedburgh into Northumberland, destroying Coquetdale and Redesdale, and burning Corbridge, Hexham and Lanercost. These expeditions were futile and inglorious efforts of retaliation. The troops returned to Jedburgh and then took possession of Dunbar Castle. Edward immediately dispatched a strong force under Warenne. The governor of the castle, Sir Richard Siward, agreed with Warenne to surrender unless he was relieved within three days. On the morning of the third day, Balliol's army came in sight, and mistaking an irregularity of movement of the English troops for a retreat, rushed upon them from a stronger position and was defeated, indeed slaughtered. Barons and squires crowded for refuge in the castle. Sir Patrick de Graham, whose valour was the unanimous admiration of Englishmen, died sword in hand. The castle surrendered next day to Edward himself, who consigned the flower of the fighting strength of Scotland to castles across England and Wales. There is reason to doubt whether Siward did not prove a traitor, and it looks as if the Scots nobles were entirely ignorant of his agreement for surrender.

Scotland lay prostrate before the invader. Having appointed constables of the eastern border castles, Edward marched on Edinburgh, which surrendered after eight days' siege. At Stirling he encountered no opposition: all had fled. Yet the record of the gaol delivery at Stirling on 19 June provides an interesting glimpse of the spirit of resistance. Thomas, the chaplain of Edinburgh, who was charged with publicly excommunicating the king with bell and candle, confessed frankly, and Richard Gulle, charged with ringing the bell, likewise confessed. Both culprits were by order of Edward delivered to the Archdeacon of Lothian.

On 7 July, in the churchyard of Stracathro, John renounced his treaty with the king of France. And on 10 July, in Brechin Castle, he formally resigned his kingdom and people, with his royal seal, to the Bishop of Durham on behalf of the king of England. There was an end of 'Toom Tabard' as king of Scotland. He was kept in England at Hertford, the Tower of London and elsewhere until 18 July 1299, when he was delivered by Sir Robert de Burghersh, Constable of Dover, to the Papal Nuncio, Reynaud, Bishop of Vincenza, at Wissant in France 'for disposal by his Holiness'. He lived to hear of the decisive victory of Bannockburn.

From the middle of March onwards to autumn, homage was paid throughout the length and breadth of Scotland to Edward and his representatives. Edward himself passed north to Elgin and after a triumphal progress of twenty-one weeks returned to Berwick on 22 August. He appointed John de Warenne, Earl of Surrey and Sussex, Governor of Scotland, Sir Hugh de Cressingham, Treasurer and Sir William de Ormsby, Justiciar. He committed the subordinate wardenships, castles and sheriffdoms to English officers. He made arrangements for the establishment of a new Treasury at Berwick on the model of the Treasury at Westminster. He broke in pieces the ancient Great Seal of Scotland and substituted a new seal. He had enforced his 'property and possession' of the realm of Scotland, yet he left behind him the active germs of retribution.

Among Edward's plunder were two notable national possessions. One was the Black or Holy Rood, 'a certified fragment of the true Cross preserved in a shrine of gold or silver gilt'. It had been brought over by St Margaret who left it as a sacred legacy to her descendants and their realm. The other, an even more honoured possession, was the Stone of Destiny – 'the palladium of Scotland'. It was reputed to have been Jacob's pillow when he saw the vision of the angels ascending and descending the ladder and to have been brought to

41

Scotland by the eponymous Scota, the daughter of Pharaoh. It was enshrined in the coronation chair of the kings of Scotland. Edward had it similarly enshrined in a chair that became the coronation throne of the kings of England. His superstition might have been overawed by the inscription:

> 'Ni fallat fatum, Scoti, quocunque locatum
> Invenient lapidem, regnare tenentur ibidem.'

That is to say:

> 'Unless the Fates are faithless grown,
>   And prophet's voice be vain,
> Where'er is found this sacred stone,
>   The Scottish race shall reign.'

For a hundred years before the death of Alexander III, the peaceful administration and firm policy of the Scottish kings had immensely strengthened Scotland both in her internal organization and in her external influence. It had inspired respect in the strongest of contemporary English sovereigns. Between Alexander III and Edward I there prevailed a genuine cordiality based not more on family relationship than on political conduct.

On the unexpected death of Alexander, the active mind of Edward must very promptly have seen a great opportunity of annexing Scotland as he had just annexed Wales. But strong-handed and imperious as he was, he was also governed by ideas of legal procedure and still more by policy. Warrior as he was, he would still prefer to attain his ends by political activity. He could not in decency raise his hand against the infant granddaughter of his own sister or arbitrarily pick a quarrel with a friendly nation at accidental disadvantage by the tragic and premature death of his amicable brother-in-law. The project of marrying the child queen to his eldest son was a stroke of policy of the happiest conception for the peaceful attainment of his purposes. The death of the queen and the rivalry of the competitors threw him on fresh lines of action, plausibly justifiable by the necessity of protecting his own kingdom from the results of internal discord on the northern border. The prolonged nature of the dispute as to the succession appears to have been very much the result of his waiting for the opening up of the smoothest line of advance. The preference of Balliol after an ostentatiously elaborate process of legal formality not only gave the appearance of a respect for the law but also placed on the throne of Scotland the candidate who would be easily manipulated. The successive steps show clearly, from the first idea of the marriage at least, the gradual and deliberate tightening of a resolute grasp upon the kingdom of Scotland.

If Edward had really believed that he was entitled to the overlordship of Scotland, it is extremely difficult to understand why he did not at once claim the wardship of the infant Margaret. The enforcement of such a claim would have been awkward enough at a moment when he needed all his force elsewhere, but he might at least have put it forward. He could not have been unaware of this right if it had actually existed. Again, as Macpherson says, 'it seems very surprising that he did not claim the crown of Scotland for himself as heir of Malcolm Kenmore, whose granddaughter Mald was his great-great-grandmother.' Such an astute intellect as his could not have been impressed with the documentary authorities arrayed by patriotic priests and supported by sycophantic officials. It is not easy to resist the conclusion that the claim was neither more nor less than a fraudulent contrivance of a semblance of legality to cover the aggression of a rapacious ambition. If the persecution of John was purely the outcome of Edward's 'exasperating legality', it does as little credit to his political capacity as the atrocity of his vengeance at Berwick and his tyrannical settlement of the conquered country.

Already, however, in the heart of an obscure young man in an obscure district of the west of Scotland there were surging turbulent feelings of personal and patriotic resentment destined eventually to overturn all these calculations of ambitious agression. That young man was William Wallace of Elderslie.

CHAPTER II

WALLACE'S FAMILY AND EARLY YEARS

'Off Scotland born, my rycht name is Wallace.'

Harry, ix 247

'At Wallace' name what Scottish blood
But boils up in a springtide flood?'

Burns

'In happy tym for Scotland thow was born.'

Harry, viii 1646.

William Wallace was the second son of Sir Malcolm Wallace of Elderslie and of his wife, Margaret, daughter of Sir Reginald Crawford of Crosby, hereditary Sheriff of Ayr.

Blind Harry, an ardent Scot himself, was extremely keen to press the fact that Wallace was a thorough Scotsman – 'of whole lineage and true line of Scotland'. Sir Malcolm, he says, at his marriage,

'Elderslie then had in heritage,
Auchinbothie, and other sundry place.
The great-grandson he was of good Wallace,
The which Wallace full worthily then wrought
When Walter her of Wales from Warin sought.'

And for further information he refers to the history of 'the right line of the first Steward'. He does not pursue the female line.

There is abundant evidence of the connection of the Wallaces with the Stewards of Scotland. Walter Fitz Alan, the first Steward, came from Oswestry in Shropshire where his father, Alan, son of Flaald, a Norman, had obtained considerable lands from William the Conqueror and had married a daughter of Warin, the sheriff of the county. He was appointed Steward of the royal household by David I who also assigned him extensive lands in Ayr and Renfrew. He would be followed to Scotland by families of local descent who would settle under him in Kyle. A Richard Walense, who witnessed charters of Walter, is found at Riccarton (Ricard-tun). Two more Richards follow, contemporary with the next three Stewards, the third Richard witnessing charters of the fourth Steward extending the territorial possessions of the family. At the head of the Elderslie branch appears a Henry Walense, supposed to be a brother of the first Richard, holding the lands of Elderslie under the first Steward. An Adam Walense, possibly a son of Henry, is found in connection with the third and fourth Stewards, and this Adam has been supposed to be the father of Sir Malcolm. The lands of Auchinbothie in Lochwinnoch were acquired by a Wallace of Elderslie.

It does not seem possible on the available evidence to place the known members of the Riccarton and Elderslie lines – if indeed they were parallel lines – in their definite positions of relationship except with the caution of probability. Harry makes Sir Richard Wallace of Riccarton the uncle of his hero, William Wallace of Elderslie, but the use of the word uncle may be definite or lax. All that can be confidently confirmed is that all these Wallaces of Riccarton, Elderslie, Auchinbothie and 'other sundry place' belonged to the same family and that, at the birth of the hero, that family had been settled in Scotland for more than a full century.

The family of Crawford is traced back to Thorlongus, an Anglo-Danish chief who was driven out of Northumberland by William the Conqueror and obtained lands in the Merse from Edgar about the beginning of the twelfth century. Early in the thirteenth century at any rate, a Sir Reginald Crawford married the heiress of Loudon and was created first hereditary Sheriff of Ayr and his grandson in the main line was the father of Margaret Crawford, the wife of Sir Malcolm Wallace. It may be confidently accepted that on both the male and female lines William Wallace's ancestors were domiciled Scots for more than a hundred years before he was born.

The ultimate origin of the Wallace family becomes unimportant. It has been suggested that the very name shows that the family was Welsh or Celtic, that the name 'was used of the Wallaces, or Welsh, of Elderslie, or elsewhere, not so much as a surname as a description', and therefore it is often given as 'le Waleys'. It may be so but not at all necessarily. Again it is certain that Wallaces came over among the Normans, and ancestors of the Wallaces of Kyle may have come over in the train of ancestors of the Stewards. But after the lapse of a century it is really not of consequence whether the family was originally Welsh or Norman or otherwise. We do not, as did the English nobles of 1238, think of Simon de Montfort as a Frenchman. Much less then is it reasonable to consider Wallace as a foreigner, for he had behind him a hundred years of ancestry on Scottish soil and his

47

forebears were lowly enough to be associated in spirit with the people of the land far more than with the exotic barons who preserved Anglo-Norman habits and feelings by free contact with England and the English court. Wallace was undoubtedly 'of whole lineage and true line of Scotland', and through his social position he was thoroughly in touch with the national feeling.

At Elderslie, in all probability, Wallace was born. The times were perfectly quiet and it seems unlikely that his mother would have been away from her home on the occasion. Harry makes the mayor of St Johnston (Perth) speak of Wallace as 'born in to the West'.

The precise date of his birth cannot be determined with certainty. The chroniclers describe him as a young man (*juvenis*) at the battle of Stirling Bridge in 1297. The report is vague, but probably it would not have been used at all unless it had been intended to mark the fact that his youthfulness was particularly striking. Harry is definite – doubly definite – but he is also contradictory. He is, indeed, emphatic on the point of Wallace's youth, but he gives two violently conflicting statements without supplying the means of making a confident decision in favour of either.

In the first place, early in his poem, Harry makes Wallace eighteen when he killed young Selby at Dundee. The date he intends is evidently about December or January 1296–97. This would make Wallace about nineteen at Stirling Bridge – an age incredible to many, although in our opinion not very difficult to accept. The Selby episode, however, may readily be thrown back to 1291–92, in which case Wallace would have been of the more mature age of twenty-three or twenty-four at Stirling Bridge while still his youth would be distinctive enough for it to be remarked upon. This age was accepted by the Marquess of Bute who placed Wallace's birth in 1274, and it is an age that would still favour the Marquess's impression that Wallace's extreme youth 'was one of the reasons for a shyness with which he was associated by many of the more leading among his own countrymen.'

In the next place, however, towards the end of his poem, Harry expressly states that Wallace was said to be forty-five when he was betrayed to the English, and here he seems to rely specifically on Blair and Gray on whose chronicle of Wallace's deeds he professes to base his poem. In xi, 1425–8, he says:

> 'Thir twa knew best off gud Schir Wilzhamys deid,
> Fra xvi zer quhill xxixty zeid.
> xl and v off age Wallace was cauld
> That tym that he was to [the] Southron sauld.'

Now, if Wallace was forty-five in 1305, he would have been born in 1260 and would have been thirty-seven at Stirling Bridge; but then he would hardly have been described as young; nor does forty-five fit in with Harry's previous chronology which ought also to agree with Blair's record. Carrick makes a desperate effort at reconciliation by suggesting that the transcriber of Harry wrote 'forty' instead of 'thirty'. However, there remains a difficulty – twenty-nine years back from 1305 brings us to 1276, some ten years before the death of Alexander III, and during this decade, as well as for at least five years later, there was profound peace and there could have been no 'deid' of Wallace's for Blair and Gray to know.

Harry might be taken to say that Blair and Gray knew Wallace from his sixteenth year until he was about twenty-nine. If he was in his thirtieth year in 1305, he would have been born in 1275. If he killed Selby in 1291–92, he would have been in his seventeenth year, which is close to Harry's statement, and at Stirling Bridge he would have been in his twenty-third year.

The date of Wallace's birth becomes movable according to the reader. At twenty-two or twenty-three Wallace must undoubtedly have been a man of exceptional (or at any rate impressive) physique, commanding energy of mind and magnetic enthusiasm. More than that, he must have been at least as experienced a soldier as any Scot in the army on the slope of Abbey Craig. Wallace may be taken to have been born in 1274 or 1275.

Wallace had certainly one brother, Malcolm, who was older than himself, possibly another brother, John, and perhaps two sisters. It is recorded in a letter written on 20 August 1299, that at the meeting of Scots barons at Peebles on the previous day, Sir Malcolm Wallace and Sir David de Graham drew their knives on each other over a demand of the latter for the lands of Sir William Wallace who was going out of the kingdom without leave. The accuracy of the writer almost conclusively bars the supposition that he could have blundered on the name Malcolm instead of John, as has been suggested. If this is so, it supports Wyntoun's statement that the 'elder brother enjoyed the heritage,' and negates Harry's assertion that young Sir Malcolm was killed with his father at Loudon Hill in 1296 – or rather in 1291. Bower mistakenly calls him Sir Andrew.

A Sir John Wallace was undoubtedly executed in London

in 1307. The sanctimonious Langtoft gloats over the details of the execution and says his head was 'raised with shouts near the head of his brother, William the Wicked' on London Bridge. It has been doubted, on no very clear grounds, whether Sir John did not belong to the family of Riccarton. Harry mentions that Wallace, during his Guardianship, 'his brother's son put to his heritage'; but this is on the presupposition that Malcolm was slain at Loudon Hill; and Sir John could hardly have been young Sir Malcolm's son. Even Langtoft may for once be right.

For the sisters there is only the authority of Harry. He mentions Edward Little as Wallace's 'sister's son', and Tom Halliday as 'sib sister's son to good Wallace'. If Harry is correct, these sisters must have been much older than Wallace.

The position of the Wallaces among the county gentry was by no means pretentious. 'I imagine them,' says the Marquess of Bute, 'in a position of easy fortune, with a certain number of free tenants paying rent in kind and services in peace, and, if need had been, in the event of war. And then with a surrounding of peasants, working at Elderslie itself and for their tenants feudally attached, paying no rent, and receiving no wages.'

As a boy, Wallace was almost certainly schooled in the elements of formal education, secular and religious, by the monks of the Abbey of Paisley, then 'the centre of religion and learning in the quasi-principality of the High Stewards, to which he belonged.' 'Taking it as a whole,' says the Marquess of Bute,

'I conceive that there can be no doubt that his mental culture was at least as great as would be that of a person in a corre-

sponding position at the present day.... Sir William Wallace at
least knew how to read and write three languages – namely,
his own, and Latin and French; and it appears also that he
knew Gaelic. He knew the ancient and modern history, and
the common simpler mathematics and science of his own day.'

In his boyhood, his deep religious feeling must also have
been powerfully fostered. The Abbey of Paisley was the parish church of his family. 'The community of Paisley,' says the
Marquess of Bute, with great probability,

> 'was then in all the fervour of its first love, and it was there
> that William Wallace imbibed his consistent and unfading
> veneration for the Church and respect for her ministers.... It
> was as the sublime compositions of the ancient Hebrew poets
> alternately thundered and wailed through the Abbey Church
> of Paisley, that William Wallace contracted that livelong love
> for the Psalms which lasted until he died, with a priest hold-
> ing the Psalter open, at his request, before his darkening eyes.'

This is probably accurate.

The foundation of Wallace's acquirements must have been
well and truly laid in his early youth. How much of his education was imparted to him at Paisley, it is quite impossible
to say. Whatever he learned there, however, must have been
powerfully reinforced by his association with an uncle, a
brother of his father's, the comfortable priest of Dunipace,
who is described by Harry as 'a man of great riches', a
'mighty parson' and 'a full kind man'. The precise period of
Wallace's stay at Dunipace cannot be pinpointed, but he
must have been well out of childhood if it is true that the
priest instilled in his pupil's mind moral maxims compactly
framed in Latin and frequently drawn from the classical

Latin authors. In particular, the good priest is credited with the noble purpose and achievement of implanting into Wallace's soul a passionate love of liberty, which is the keynote of his elevated character and his glorious career. The very formula employed to imprint the memorable injunction has been preserved for us through the centuries:

> 'Dico tibi verum, libertas optima rerum:
> Nunquam servili sub nexu vivito, fili.'

> 'My son, I tell thee soothfastlie,
> No gift is like to libertie;
> Then never live in slaverie.'

Artificial as the Latin couplet may seem, it has become invested for ever with an interest peculiarly touching to all lovers of human freedom and especially to the compatriots of Wallace.

At a still later period, according to Harry, Wallace was sent for further instruction to Dundee. The occasion of this was, in fact, the breakup of the Elderslie home. Harry reports the date as 1296, when 'Scotland was lost' after Dunbar, but he does not recognize that Scotland was lost in 1291, which seems likely to have been the true date of the episode.

On 11 June 1291, the Scots Guardians surrendered the kingdom and the castles to Edward as overlord, and on 12 June, Edward, 'with the advice of the prelates and magnates of Scotland there present', settled a general ordinance requiring 'homage and fealty to be made by all, who would have been bound to make it to a living King of Scotland.' Sir Malcolm Wallace, however, did not appear before Edward's deputies at Ayr, nor did he send an excuse. There is no evidence, indeed, to show that he ever made submission – worthy father of his heroic son! According to Harry, he retired to the Lennox, taking young Malcolm with him, while Sir Reginald Crawford, who bent to the storm as hereditary Sheriff of Ayr, took charge of Lady Wallace, his sister and the boy William, and sent them to safety to an uncle, a priest at Kilspindie in the Carse of Gowrie. Whether the priest was Sir Reginald's or Wallace's uncle is not clear, but since Harry describes him as 'an aged man', he may be taken rather as Sir Reginald's uncle. Assuming Harry's connection of events, the flight to Kilspindie must have taken place in 1296 or 1291 – preferably 1291 when Wallace was in his seventeenth year.

Sir Malcolm seems to have soon ventured back from the Lennox, if Harry is right in stating that shortly afterwards he was killed at Loudon Hill in a conflict with an English party under an officer named Fenwick. According to Harry, young Malcolm was slain with his father, which, as we have seen, is almost certainly a mistake. His desperate valour, as described by Harry, anticipates the Chevy Chace minstrel's picture of Widrington, who, 'when his legs were hewn in two, yet he kneeled and fought on his knee.' But it is curious to observe that the first edition of Harry's poem (1570), by the transposition of two lines (as compared with the existing MS.), assigns the description to Sir Malcolm the father, and no doubt this is right.

> 'His hough sinews they cuttèd in that press;
> On knees he fought, and many English slew;
> To him more fighters than enow there drew;
> On either side with spears they bore him down;
> And there they stabbed that good knight of renown.'

Meantime Wallace was living at Kilspindie and proceeding

with his studies at Dundee in a school connected with the Church. There he met John Blair, who subsequently became a Benedictine monk but left the cloister to attend his friend as chaplain, to lend a hand in many a tough fight or to conduct diplomatic negotiations, and who eventually wrote the biography that formed the basis of Harry's poem, probably in Dunfermline Abbey. There, too, according to Harry, he met Duncan of Lorn who figures in one of his early enterprises, Sir Niel Campbell of Lochawe and probably others of his later trusty comrades.

The question arises why young Wallace was staying at Kilspindie instead of accompanying his father and his brother. He must have been a big man, well capable of wielding arms. It may be that his father judged that his own and his eldest son's lives were a sufficiently heavy stake and that it was desirable that one of his sons at least should be near his wife, even in a place of comparative shelter. If it had been intended that William should rejoin his father and brother in due course, the early disaster at Loudon Hill would have rendered his presence in the west worse than futile. There may, indeed, have been another idea. There may have been an intention to dedicate him, a younger son, to the service of the Church. Harry indicates, at a late period of his career, some purpose of religious retirement 'to serve God and the Kirk' – a tendency that may readily connect itself with an early bent of mind.

The idea of making Wallace a priest, if it ever existed, was promptly dispelled by the force of circumstances. One day, Harry says, he was grossly insulted in Dundee by a young Englishman named Selby, a son of the 'Captain', who was strolling about with several companions. Wallace restrained himself until Selby attempted to take his knife from him. Wallace then seized Selby by the collar and struck him dead on the spot. Defending himself knife in hand, he made for a house his uncle had used to frequent and was quickly disguised by the lady of the house in a dress of her own. He thus eluded his pursuers and at night he escaped out of the town. The English authorities at once put the law in active motion in Dundee and made it impossible for him to remain any longer in the neighbourhood.

This episode, the very first of Harry's stories, has been overclouded with doubts. In deference to the scruples of those who cannot imagine Wallace as only at the end of his teens at Stirling Bridge, we have ventured to throw back the occurrence some five years. Who was Captain of Dundee in 1296–97 we do not know. Was Selby then the 'Captain' in 1291–92? The Captain of Dundee Castle from 18 July 1291 to 18 November 1292 was Sir Brian Fitz Alan, but Sir Brian was at the same time castellan of Forfar and (from 4 August) of Roxburgh and Jedburgh, and on 13 June he had also been appointed one of the Guardians, and he was (at any rate by 23 August) one of the three Justices. His hands must therefore have been very full of official business and he could not be always in Dundee. It has accordingly been suggested that Selby might have been his deputy, or lieutenant, in Dundee – the acting 'Captain'. But he may, on the other hand, have been the Captain, not of the castle, but of the town. Or should we suspect that 'Selby' may be a popular form of 'Fitz Alan'? The story, if accepted at all, probably dates in December 1291 or January 1292. Wallace would thus have stayed at Kilspindie about six months.

The experiences of this half-year may well have made a

profound impression upon a youth of Wallace's sensitive temperament and martial spirit. Harry represents him, with dramatic truth at least, as brooding painfully over the death of his father (and brother), and as being stirred to uncontrollable resentment of the treatment of Scots people. On Harry's statement, the desolation of his house, the exile of his mother and the oppression of his countrymen had already nerved his heart and hand to terrible reprisals – such reprisals as, apart from the controlling circumstances, would be justly deemed monstrous. Harry himself is consistently 'dispitfull and savage' against the Southron, yet one cannot but hesitate to ascribe to his bloodthirsty imagination the private deeds of revenge he attributes to young Wallace. In those hard days, the removal of an enemy did not touch the conscience as it does in modern civilized society, accustomed to peace and security and informed with a developed sense of humanity; and the justification derived from intolerable oppression is at any rate a vastly more efficient salve in the actual case than it is in mere historical contemplation. At all events, Harry relates that young Wallace, on finding an Englishman alone, never hesitated to cut his throat or to stab him dead. 'Some disappeared, but none wist by what way.' The weak, maddened by tyranny, will do as they may. There is ample testimony to the exacerbation of Scottish feeling at this period, and while we may deplore, we need not be so childishly unhistorical as to pretend not to understand. The iron of English oppression had already entered deep into the soul of Wallace.

About eighteen, then, young Wallace bore the brand of an outlaw for the shedding of English blood in peculiarly daring circumstances. The family council at Kilspindie decided that he and his mother had better travel westward again. They assumed the disguise of pilgrims to St Margaret's shrine at Dunfermline. At Dunipace they resisted the urgent invitation of the priest to stay until better times, and from there they made straight for Elderslie. Sir Reginald Crawford would have had the outlawry annulled, but Wallace was obdurate and irreconcilable. There were many Englishmen in the neighbourhood, and Sir Reginald, to get his spirited nephew out of the way of harm and of temptation, sent him to Sir Richard Wallace at Riccarton. There they kept him quiet and safe for a time – possibly until the English occupation of 1296.

At a Christmas time a few years later, when Wallace (according to Harry) was closely engaged in the far west – Harry suggests 1297, but he cannot be right – there came to him the heavy news of the death of his mother. She is said to have been compelled to leave Elderslie once more and to have returned on pilgrimage to Dunfermline to seek at the holy shrine of St Margaret the rest denied her in her own home. Unable personally to attend his mother and pay his final respects, Wallace dispatched John Blair and the sturdy Jop to represent him on the mournful occasion. The bitterness of his heart is expressed by Harry in two lines:

'Better him thought that it had happened so;
No Southron should her put to other woe.'

Still more distressing was the fate of Wallace's wife, Marion Bradfute, the heiress of Lamington. Wyntoun calls her his 'leman' (sweetheart) – a designation not necessarily contradictory but at least ambiguous. Harry's account agrees with Wyntoun's very closely, yet he would seem to have had

58

some other narrative before him, and possibly Wyntoun and Harry may have drawn upon a common predecessor. However this may be, Harry, with inflexible allegiance to his hero, affirms: 'Mine author says she was his rightwise wife.' The point really needs no consideration.

Harry lavishes a wealth of tender emotion over the loves of Wallace and Marion Bradfute, and his sympathetic feeling elevates him to genuine poetic expression, often touched with extreme delicacy. Marion lived at Lanark, 'a maiden mild' of eighteen. Her father, Sir Hugh de Bradfute, and her eldest brother had been slain by Hazelrig, the Sheriff of Lanark. Her mother, too, was dead, and such peace as she enjoyed was dependent on her having 'purchased King Edward's protection', although that did not secure her from the offensive attentions of his local minions.

> 'Amiable and benign she was, and wise,
> Courteous and sweet, fulfilled of gentrice,
> Her tongue well ruled, her face right fresh and fair.
> Withal she was a maid of virtue rare:
> Humbly her led, and purchased a good name,
> And kept herself with every wight from blame.
> True rightwise folk great favour did her lend.'

When Wallace first saw her, Hazelrig had just broached a proposal of marriage between her and his son. Harry dwells strongly on the division of Wallace's mind between the claims of war and the urgency of love, and he tells how the faithful Kerly's pointed advice broke down his hesitations. The inevitable conflict with Hazelrig arose. The sheriff's emissaries fastened a quarrel on Wallace. Taken at a disadvantage, he was compelled to retreat to his house. His wife, having admitted him and his men, and let them out by another way, held the pursuers in parley until his escape was assured. Whether then or immediately after (on Hazelrig's return to town), she paid for her courageous fidelity with her life. Wallace, with a handful of men, came upon Hazelrig at dead of night and slew him in his bedroom with his own hand. The Lanark rising and the death of the sheriff certainly took place in May 1297.

Harry further asserts that a daughter was born to Wallace and his wife, that she married a squire named Shaw and that 'right goodly men came of this lady young.' The edition of 1594 at this point inserts a few lines not found in the existing manuscript, stating that this daughter of Wallace's married a squire of 'Balliol's blood' and that:

'their heirs by line succeeded right
To Lamington and other lands of worth.'

This points to an alleged second marriage with Sir William Baillie of Hoprig. To this allegation it is by no means a conclusive answer that Sir William Baillie, second of Hoprig, as son-in-law of Sir William Seton, obtained a charter of 'Lambiston' barony as late as 1368.

According to Harry's narrative, Wallace found some of his most active and trustworthy allies, especially in his earlier career, among his own relatives. This is at least extremely probable. Sir Richard Wallace of Riccarton gives him food and shelter and sends him his three sons, of whom Adam, the eldest, distinguishes himself conspicuously. The priests of Dunipace and Kilspindie we have already met. Wallace of Auchincruive, 'his cousin', provides supplies for the outlaw of Laglane Wood and his single 'child'. Edward Little is

Wallace's 'sister's son'. Tom Halliday, too, is Wallace's 'nephew' – his 'sib sister's son', and Halliday's eldest daughter is the wife of Wallace's great lieutenant, Sir John the Graham, while his second daughter is the wife of Johnstone, 'a man of good degree', installed as castellan of Lochmaben, the first castle that Wallace attempted to hold permanently. Young Auchinleck of Gilbank becomes Wallace's 'eyme' or 'uncle', by marriage. Kirkpatrick is 'of kin' and to 'Wallace' mother near'. Kneland (or Cleland) and William Crawford are both designated his 'cousins'; Kneland, indeed, his 'near cousin'. The family tree must have thrown out shoots in many directions and more likely than not Harry may be substantially right.

Wallace, as we have seen, and as the indictment on his trial stated, was a Scotsman born and bred. His ancestors on both sides, whether Celtic, Norman or Saxon, had been domiciled in Scotland for more than a century and had entered into the feeling and thought of the mass of the Scots population. Wallace himself, possibly with a view to the Church, had received as good an education as the times afforded. Whether or not the good priest of Dunipace inculcated in his opening mind the inestimable value of liberty, he was aroused, while yet 'in his tender age', to bitter reprisals on the oppressors of his family and of his countrymen. A younger son, without rank or fortune or the experience of age, he girded on his sword 'both sharp and long' and appealed to the justice of Heaven. Scorning intercession for relief of his outlawry, he took himself to the fastnesses of his country, resolute to right his wrongs in the only way open to him, and filled with undying hatred for the tyrants of his native land.

CHAPTER III

GUERRILLA WARFARE

'Unus homo nobis cunctando restituit rem.' –
Enn. *ap*. Cic. *Off.* i. 24, 84
'Now, for our consciences, the arms are fair,
When the intent of bearing them is just.' –
Shakespeare, *Henry IV*, Part I, v. 2
'Thryldome is weill wer than deid.' –
Barbour, *The Bruce*, i. 269

Apart from the Hazelrig and Ormsby episodes, the chroniclers place Wallace at Stirling Bridge almost as if he had appeared from nowhere, ready to command an army in the
field. Yet they call him a brigand, public robber, cut-throat
and other names, all strangely inadequate as an explanation
of his command of the Scots against a mighty English host.
Wallace's leadership really has to be accounted for on some
more rational principle.

Now, Harry is the main guide up to the Hazelrig episode,
and Harry has been grievously discredited. As the criticism
of his poem stands, each reader must be left free to make his
or her own deductions, but at least it may be claimed for
Harry that each episode be judged on its merits, not by the
jeers of Lord Hailes or an echo thereof. In any case, it is be-

yond all question that Wallace must have gone through some such experience as Harry details. Stirling Bridge was not a miracle of history.

Occasional Early Adventures

It might be possible to refer some of the earlier exploits of Wallace, as recorded by Harry, to 1292 without much more violence than is involved in the like reference of the Selby episode. But there is no similar necessity. They all imply the presence of Sir Henry de Percy in the Ayr district, and Percy was appointed Warden of Galloway and Ayr and Castellan of Ayr, Wigton, Cruggelton and Buittle on 8 September 1296 although he did not reach his post until well into October of that year.

What Wallace had been doing in the period between 1292 and 1296 remains unknown. It seems hopeless to connect him in any way with the events of March and April 1296 at Berwick and Dunbar, and it is likely enough that Sir Richard Wallace carefully kept him out of mischief and danger at Riccarton until the fresh occupation of Galloway and Ayr by the English in October 1296. On the assumption, however, of his marriage with Marion Bradfute, which cannot easily be placed later than the first months of 1296, there must have been considerable intermissions of his restraint. Sir Reginald Crawford had duly submitted to Edward, who confirmed him in the Sheriffdom of Ayr on 14 May at Roxburgh.

The fresh involvement of Wallace with the English is ascribed by Harry to an accidental conflict with five of Percy's men at the Water of Irvine. Wallace was fishing as Percy passed and the men proceeded to confiscate his catch. He killed three of the five. Sir Richard was distracted. Plainly, Wallace could not remain any longer at Riccarton. Taking a youth as his sole attendant, he rode straight to Wallace of Auchincruive and sought shelter in Laglane Wood where his relative secretly supplied him with provisions.

Wallace, however, was fustrated by inaction. He left his place of safety and ventured to Ayr. At the market cross he fell in with a champion who was offering English soldiers and others a stroke on his back with a rough bucket pole for a groat. Wallace gave him three groats, delivered his stroke and broke the man's backbone. The English at once attacked him, and he had to kill five of them before he could escape to his horse which he had left with his man at the edge of the wood.

This affair having blown over, Wallace would again visit Ayr. It was market day. Sir Reginald's servant had bought fish when Percy's steward demanded them, and on Wallace's intervention, the steward struck him with his hunting staff. Wallace instantly collared him and stabbed him in the heart: 'caterer thereafter, sure, he was no more.' Some eighty men-at-arms had been assigned to keep order on market day, and Wallace was at once surrounded. After a fierce struggle, with many casualties, he was taken prisoner – 'to pine him more' than outright death. Cast into a cell and badly fed, he fell very ill, and when the gaoler was sent down to bring him up for judgment, he reported his prisoner apparently dead. The result was that Wallace's body was tossed over the wall into 'a draff midden', presumed lifeless. Hearing of this, his old nurse, who lived in the new town of Ayr, begged to take the body away for burial, and her request granted, she had it carried to her house. Her attendance revived Wallace, but she kept up the outward pretence that he was dead. It argues a good nurse and a good constitution if he made recovery within the limits of time indicated by Harry.

At this period the famous poet Thomas the Rhymer happened to be on a visit at the neighbouring monastery of Faile (St Mary's). He felt deep concern for Wallace's fate. The 'Minister' of the house dispatched a messenger to establish the truth privately. On hearing that Wallace was really alive,

> 'Then Thomas said: "For sooth, ere he decease,
> Shall many thousands in the field make end.
> From Scotland he shall forth the Southron send,
> And Scotland thrice he shall bring to the peace.
> So good of hand again shall ne'er be kenned."'

A similar prophecy is mentioned by Harry as lying heavy on the mind of Percy – a prophecy that a Wallace should turn the English out of Scotland. 'Wise men,' said Percy, 'the sooth by his escape may see.' The same view, according to Harry, took a strong hold of the popular mind.

Sending his benefactress and her family to his mother at Elderslie, Wallace got hold of a rusty sword and set out for Riccarton. On the way he encountered an English squire named Longcastell (Lancaster) with two men who insisted on taking him to Ayr. Wallace pleaded to be let alone for he was sick. Longcastell disagreed and drew his sword. Wallace at once struck him dead with his rusty weapon and then killed the two followers. Taking the spoils, he hurried to Riccarton. Sir Reginald and Wallace's mother and many friends then came and a great celebration ensued.

Guerrilla in the West

Wallace, however, would not rest at Riccarton. He was helped with his preparations and was accompanied by several spirited lads, his relatives and friends. Adam Wallace, Sir Richard's eldest son, now eighteen, Robert Boyd, Kneland, 'near cousin to Wallace', Edward Little 'his sister's son', and Gray and Kerly, with some attendants, rode with him to Mauchline Moor. Learning there that an English convoy from Carlisle to Ayr was approaching, Wallace rode to Loudon Hill and lay in wait. The convoy came in sight. It was conducted by Fenwick, the officer who had commanded the English in the recent combat here when Wallace's father was slain. This set of circumstances exalted Wallace's spirit and steeled his mind to a resolute revenge. He had but 50 men against 180 and his men fought on foot. By throwing up a rough dyke of stones, he had narrowed the approach of the harnessed English horse whose riders fancied they had no more to do than to trample their enemies down. Wallace promptly disabused their minds of that time-honoured superciliousness. His men plied them first with spears and then with swords, keeping close order and defying the horsemen's efforts to scatter them. Wallace himself in fury struck Fenwick from his horse, Boyd giving the finishing blow, and a hundred of the English lay dead on the field. The superstition of the invincibility of armed horse by footmen was exploded by Wallace's tactics and fierce resolution. The victors carried off Percy's convoy to the depths of the forest of Clydesdale whence they freely distributed 'stuff and horses' privately to friendly neighbours. The success of this daring effort tended to corroborate the prophecy of True Thomas and spread the fame of Wallace.

Wallace's Loudon Hill exploit came under the jurisdiction of Percy in council at Glasgow. Sir Reginald was made responsible for the culprit's good behaviour, and in order to shield the Sheriff, Wallace's comrades induced him to consent to a peace for ten months – a peace limited to Percy's jurisdiction. Presently Wallace would yet again see Ayr, where he went with fifteen men. Invited by an English buckler-player to try his sword, Wallace cut through buckler, hand and brain down to the shoulders. At once a fight ensued at great odds, and the Scots had to retire, Wallace protecting the rear. Harry says 29 out of 120 English, including three of Percy's near kin, were slain. Percy, however, recognized that Wallace was not the aggressor and contented himself with ordering Sir Reginald to keep him from the market town and fairs and like resorts. So, for a week or two Wallace stayed at Crosby.

Another Council was now summoned at Glasgow 'to statute the country.' Sir Reginald, as sheriff, obeyed the summons, taking Wallace with him. Wallace rode ahead, overtaking the sheriff's baggage which soon caught up with Percy's. Percy's horse was tired and Sir Reginald's fresher horse was appropriated despite Wallace's protests. Sir Reginald took it very calmly. Wallace, however, fired up and swore that peace or no peace, please the sheriff or otherwise, he would exact amends for the wrong. Spurring forward again in high dudgeon, with Gray and Kerly by his side, he quickly overtook Percy's baggage east of Cathcart, slew the five attendants and took the spoil. Then said Wallace, 'At some strength would I be.'

The Council promptly outlawed Wallace and made Sir Reginald swear to have no further contact with him. Meantime Wallace with his two men had passed to the Lennox. Harry sends him to Earl Malcolm who proposed to make him 'master of his household'. The Earl had, in fact, already sworn fealty to Edward, not once, but twice (14 March and 28 August), although Harry says, 'he had not then made band'; but that consideration would be open to easy interpretation in the remote fastnesses of Dumbartonshire. In any case, Wallace is said to have declined the offer, his mind being set upon wreaking revenge on the English. He was joined by about sixty men, some of them Irish exiles, and all of them pretty rough. Two of them of note: Fawdon, a big dour fellow, and Steven of Ireland, a most valuable recruit who soon became a great friend of Kerly's.

> 'Wallace received what man would come him till;
> The bodily oath they made him with good will
> Before the Earl, all with a good accord,
> And him received as captain and their lord.'

Gray and Kerly who had been with him at Loudon Hill he instructed to keep near his person, knowing them 'right hardy, wise, and true'. The field of action was closed against him in the west. He would therefore strike to the north.

Guerrilla in the North

With his sixty men, Wallace started through the Lennox. He was well provided from the spoil of Percy's baggage, and he liberally distributed the good earl's gifts among his followers. The first exploit of the campaign was the capture of the peel of Gargunnock, a little west of Stirling. Wallace sent two spies at midnight to find out how the place was defended and their report was that security was slack – sentry asleep, bridge down, labourers going in without question. Moving in with due caution, Wallace entered without hindrance. The peel door he found guarded with a stubborn bar, which, to the marvel of his men, he wrenched out with his hands, bringing three yards' breadth of the wall with it. Next moment, he burst in the door with his foot. The watchman, wakened up suddenly, struck at him with 'a felon staff of steel' which Wallace wrested out of his hands and brained him with. The captain, Thirlwall, with the aroused garrison at his heels, came forward, only to be battered to death with the same steel mace. Not a single fighting man – and there were twenty-two of them – was spared, but women and children, according to Wallace's invariable rule, were protected. Having gathered the spoils, Wallace and his men hastened on their way.

Crossing the Forth, they headed north to the Teith, where Wallace gave Kerly custody of the useful mace of steel, and having passed the Teith, they held on by one 'strength' and another to Strathearn, religiously slaying every Englishman they came across. At Blackford, for instance, they encountered five riding to Doune, and killed and spoiled them and put the bodies 'out of sight'. They then crossed the Earn and made for Methven Wood where they found 'a land of great abundance'.

Wallace, however, did not enjoy the fat of the forest in idleness. He longed to see St Johnston (Perth). Appointing Steven of Ireland, who had done good service as guide after Gargunnock, to command in his absence, Wallace took seven men and set off to the town.

'What is your name?' inquired the provost (mayor).

'Will Malcolmson,' replied Wallace, 'from Ettrick Forest, and I want to find a better dwelling in this north land.'

The provost recited the rumours that were rife about Wallace, the outlaw.

'I hear speak of that man,' said Wallace, 'but tidings of him can I tell you none.'

Sir Gerard Heron was captain, and 'under-captain' was Sir John Butler, son of Sir James Butler of Kinclaven, who then happened to be in St Johnston. Harry recounts Wallace's nightly regrets that he had not force enough to take the town. He discovered, however, the strength and distribution of the enemy in these parts, and, having learnt when Sir James Butler was to return to Kinclaven, he at once set out again for Methven Wood where the blast of his well-known horn quickly assembled his men.

Advancing towards Kinclaven, on the right bank of the Tay a little above the junction of the Isla, Wallace distributed his men near the castle in a thickly wooded hollow. In the early afternoon his scouts brought him the news that three fore-riders had passed, but he did not move until Butler and his train came up so as to make sure of their exact strength. There were ninety men on horseback. When Wallace showed himself, these warriors contemptuously imagined they could simply ride down him and his footmen, but they were promptly taught the lesson of Loudon Hill. Wallace and his men stood shoulder to shoulder and plied their swords with devastating effect. Wallace himself was conspicuous, and at length he reached Sir James Butler and clove him to the teeth. Steven of Ireland and Kerly 'with his good staff of steel' especially distinguished themselves. Sixty of Butler's men were slain, and the remnant fled to the castle, hotly pursued by the Scots. The bridge was lowered and the gates cast open to the fugitives, but Wallace followed so fast that he got command of the gate and his men entered with the fleeing enemy. Not a fighting man was left alive in the place; only Lady Butler and her women, two priests and the children were spared. Only five Scots were killed. Having plundered, dismantled and burnt the castle, Wallace withdrew into Shortwood Shaw.

When the country folk, seeing the smoke, approached Kinclaven Castle, they found 'but walls and stone'. Lady Butler herself carried the news to St Johnston. At once Sir Gerard Heron ordered 1000 men, 'harnessed on horse into their armour clear', to pursue Wallace. The force was disposed in six equal companies, five to surround the wood; the sixth, led by Sir John Butler, to make the direct attack. Wallace had taken up a strong position which he fortified by crossbars of trees except on one side, whence he could issue to the open ground. This 'strength' he determined must be held to the last. Butler had 140 archers, said to be Lancashire men, with 80 spears in support. Wallace had only 20 archers, and 'few of them were sikker [sure] of archery' – they were more familiar with spear and sword. Wallace himself had a bow of Ulysses: 'no man was there that Wallace' bow might draw.' He was short of arrows, however, for when he had shot fifteen, his stock was exhausted. The English, on the other hand, were plentifully supplied. The odds were overwhelmingly in their favour. Wallace did his utmost to shelter his men 'and cast all ways to save them from the death'. With his own hand he dealt death to many of the foe in sudden sallies. Here he had a very narrow escape. Observing his tactics, an English archer lay in wait for him and shot him:

> 'Under the chin, through a collar of steel,
> On the left side, and hurt his neck some deal.'

It is curious to note that the alleged French description of Wallace preserved by Harry mentions 'a wen' or scar in this very spot. Wallace instantly made directly for his assailant at all hazards and killed him in sight of friends and foes.

In the course of the afternoon the English were reinforced by the arrival of Sir William de Loraine from Gowrie with 300 men to avenge the death of his uncle, Sir James Butler.

'Here is no choice,' said Wallace, 'but either do or die.'

A combined assault was made on his position by Butler and Loraine and he had only 50 to withstand 500. The battle raged fiercely, and in spite of his most arduous efforts with his 'burly brand', Wallace was compelled to evacuate and to seek shelter in the thickest part of the wood. At last he cut his way through Butler's company and established himself in another 'strength'. The English stuck close to him, however. In the melee, he struck hard at Butler who was saved from death by the interposition of the bough of a tree which Wallace brought down upon him. By this time Loraine had come up, and Wallace, making straight at him, cut him down but did not regain the 'strength' without a desperate struggle.

> 'The worthy Scots right nobly did that day
> About Wallace, till he was won away.'

Still Wallace held his 'strength'. Sir Gerard Heron, however, on hearing of the death of Loraine, moved all his troops simultaneously against the position; whereupon Wallace and his men issued at the north side of the wood in retreat, 'thanking great God' that they got off on such terms. The Scots had lost seven men killed; the English, 120.

Wallace took refuge in Cargill Wood. The English, deeming it fruitless to pursue him, set about seeking where the plunder of Kinclaven had been deposited in the forest; but they found nothing except Sir James's horse. They then returned to St Johnston more dispirited than elated. The second night, the Scots returned cautiously to Shortwood Shaw and carried away the hidden spoils. By sunrise they reached Methven Wood and three days afterwards they established themselves in a strength in Elcho Park. They had eluded the vigilance of their enemies.

Thanks to the temerity of Wallace, however, they were soon discovered. According to Harry, he returned to St Johnston disguised as a priest to pursue a former amour. He was recognized and watched, and the woman is said to have disclosed the date of the next meeting. He was accordingly waylaid, but when she confessed, he threw aside his own disguise, arrayed himself in her dress and managed to pass safely out at the gate. As he increased his pace, two of the guards, thinking him 'a stalwart quean' (girl) hastened after him. In a few minutes they lay dead on the South Inch and Wallace was hurrying to Elcho Park. This story of Harry's is unusually clumsy or the eyes of the guards must have been peculiarly vacant.

The two men being found slain on the South Inch, Sir Gerard Heron set out in pursuit of Wallace with 600 men. He took with him also a sleuth-hound of the best Border breed. Heron with half his force surrounded the wood where Wallace was posted and Butler made the attack with the rest, 300 against 40. In the first ruthless onset, the Scots killed 40 but lost fifteen. Finding their ground untenable, they cut their way through the enemy to the banks of the Tay, intending to cross, but the water was deep and one half of them could not swim. They had no alternative, therefore, but to face Butler's men again, and after a severe struggle, in which Steven and Kerly, as well as Wallace, performed heroic deeds, they again cut through the English, killing 60 and losing nine. Already Wallace had lost more than half his men, twenty-four out of 40, and sixteen was a mere handful against hundreds. As Butler was re-forming his men, Wallace took the opportunity to dash through between him and Heron and made for Gask Wood.

The approach of night was in his favour. But the way was uphill and rough, and when they were still east of Dupplin, a considerable distance from the anticipated shelter, Fawdon broke down and would not be persuaded to hurry on. Having exhausted argument and entreaty, Wallace in anger struck off his head. Harry justifies the act. It might stop the sleuth-hound. Fawdon was suspected of treachery; he was 'right stark' (strong) and had gone only a short distance. If he was false, he would join the enemy; if he was true, the enemy would kill him. 'Might he do aught but lose him as it was?' On the alleged facts, probably there is little more to be said. The succeeding narrative shows plainly enough that Wallace felt himself to be in a most painful dilemma.

While Wallace hastened forward, Steven and Kerly stayed behind in a bushy hollow until Heron came up, and then cautiously mixed with the English as they were speculating on Fawdon's fate. The hound had stopped, and as Heron was inspecting Fawdon, Kerly suddenly struck him dead. Kerly and Steven at once dashed off towards the Earn. Butler dispatched an escort with Heron's body to St Johnston and pushed on to Dalreoch. Meantime Wallace had occupied Gask Hall – Baroness Nairne's 'Bonny Gascon Ha'' –

'an unco tow'r, sae stern an' auld' –

with his remnant of fourteen men and was painfully anxious about Steven and Kerly, and vexed about the death of Fawdon. In the circumstances of his mental excitement and bodily fatigue, the story of the apparition of Fawdon, which Harry works up so elaborately, finds a very natural basis. Whether or not Wallace sent out his men in relays to discover the meaning of the strange horn blowing, and so forth, and then ventured out alone under the urgency of the apparition, he appears to have now lost all touch with his men.

Passing along Earnside all alone, Wallace came upon Sir John Butler who was patrolling the fords. Butler, suspecting his explanation of his business, drew his sword, whereupon Wallace killed him, seized his horse and rode away pursued hotly by the English. In the running fight he killed some twenty of them, but at Blackford his horse collapsed and he was obliged to take to the heather on foot. Struggling to the Forth, he swam the cold river and hastened to the Torwood where he got shelter in a widow's hut. Sending out messengers to get news of his men, he retired to a deep thicket to rest watched by two of the widow's sons, while a third went to inform the priest of Dunipace of his arrival.

The priest came. Wallace was still suffering severely from fatigue as well as excitement.

> 'What I have had in war before this day –
> Prison and pain – to this night was but play. . . .
> I moan far more the losing of my men
> Than for myself, had I ten times such pain.'

The priest, however ardent for freedom in the abstract, could not but recognize the hopelessness of Wallace's position. His men were lost; more would not rise with him in their place; it was useless for him to throw away his life. Let him seek honourable terms with Edward. The old man may have been overpowered by Wallace's disastrous condition; he may have been testing his nephew's mettle.

> "'Uncle," said Wallace, "of such words no more.
> This is but eking of my trouble sore.
> Better I like to see the Southron dee
> Than land or gold that they can give to me.
> Believe right well, from war I will not cease
> Till time that I bring Scotland into peace,
> Or die therefor: that plainly understand."'

Such was the indomitable resolution of Wallace in these hopeless circumstances. Presently he was cheered by the arrival of Steven and Kerly who were overjoyed to find him alive. 'For perfect joy they wept with all their een.' Wallace was eager to move. The widow gave him 'part of silver bright' and two of her sons. She would have given the third but he was too young. The priest provided Wallace with horses and clothing, but 'wae he was his mind was all in war.' And so Wallace passed on to Dundaff Moor. Although the northern campaign had closed with the annihilation of his force, it had spread the rumour and inflamed the spirit of resistance.

The Capture of Lochmaben

Wallace with his four followers rode to Dundaff, a hilly tract in Stirlingshire. The lord of Dundaff, according to Harry, was Sir John the Graham, 'an aged knight' who paid tribute for a quiet life. Abercrombie, however, following Sympson, says he belonged not to the Dundaff but to the Abercorn family, and, on the strength of a charter in the possession of the Duke of Montrose, he states that Dundaff was then held by Sir David de Graham. A Sir David de Graham, brother of the gallant Sir Patrick, was taken prisoner at Dunbar and relegated to St Briavell's Castle. Anyhow, this knight of Dundaff had a son, also named Sir John, 'both wise, worthy, and wight', and

> 'On a broad shield his father gart him swear
> He would be true to Wallace in all thing,
> And he to him while life might in them ryng' (reign).

Young Sir John prepared to ride with Wallace, but Wallace would not take him then.

> 'A plain part yet I will not take on me.
> I have lost men through my o'er-reckless deed:
> A burnt child will the fire more sorely dread.'

He would try to raise his friends in Clydesdale and give Sir John notice. Sir John eventually became his most notable lieutenant.

So Wallace passed on to Bothwell Moor, to one Crawford, no doubt a relative, and next day he went to Gilbank which was held on tribute by Auchinleck, a youth of nineteen, closely related to him by marriage. Here he is said to have remained over Christmas. The English in these parts had heard of his activities in the north, but he had disappeared in Strathearn and so went out of their minds. Wallace, although lying quiet, was not inactive. He dispatched the trusty Kerly to Sir Reginald, Boyd, Blair and Adam of Riccarton. Blair at once visited him. From all his friends reinforcements poured into his exchequer.

> 'All true Scots then great favour to him gave:
> What good they had he needed not to crave.'

Starting from Gilbank after Christmas, Wallace with his four men rode to Corheid in Annandale. Here he was joined by Tom Halliday and Edward Little, who were delighted to find that there was no truth in the report that he had been slain in Strathearn. Wallace was now sixteen. He longed to see Lochmaben town. So he set out with Halliday, Edward and Kerly, leaving the rest in the Knock Wood. While they were hearing mass, Clifford, Percy's nephew, with four men, came to their hostelry and spitefully cut off the tails of their horses. Wallace killed them all. The English quickly pursued, about 150 strong. Wallace reached his men in the Knock Wood, but his horses were failing through loss of blood and he was caught up before gaining Corheid. Turning again desperately, he killed fifteen of the leading pursuers and compelled the survivors to fall back on the main body but did not pursue, Halliday having discovered some 200 in ambush. The English again pressed the Scots' retreat. Wallace cut down the redoubtable Sir Hugh de Morland and, mounting Morland's 'courser wight', again compelled the advanced guard to retire with the loss of twenty men. Sir John de Graystock, the English leader, was furious. Meantime Wallace hurried on, himself and Halliday stoutly guarding the rear.

Near Queensberry, Wallace was happily reinforced by Sir John the Graham with thirty men and by Kirkpatrick of Torthorwald who had been holding out in Eskdale Wood with twenty men. The Scots thereupon charged through the English, scattering them in flight, but 100 held together, and Wallace, with brusque directness, recalled Sir John and ordered him to break up this body. The rout was complete, and at the Knock Head Sir John killed Graystock. The valour of Sir John, Kirkpatrick and Halliday had been conspicuous. Harry remarks a delicate courtesy of Wallace's in apologizing to Sir John for the brusqueness of his order in the heat of the pursuit; and no less generous was Sir John's answer. In this engagement the Scots did not lose a single man!

The victorious Scots now held a council and unanimously adopted Wallace's proposal to take Lochmaben Castle, the seat of the Bruce. The possession of Lochmaben would establish a strong footing against the English, and perhaps they might also link with it Carlaverock Castle, if this could be wrested from Sir Herbert de Maxwell. In the dusk of the evening, Halliday, taking with him John Watson, both of them having special local knowledge, rode to the gate. The porter, who knew Watson well, unsuspiciously opened the gate on his information that the captain was coming and was instantly killed by Halliday, Watson taking his keys. Wallace then came up and entered, finding only women and a couple of menservants. The women he spared, but the men he killed. As the Knock Head fugitives returned, Watson let them in and Wallace's men immediately slew them. 'No man left there that was of England born.' Johnstone, the husband of Halliday's second daughter – probably the Johnstone of Eskdale mentioned later by Harry – was made captain. Lochmaben was thus the first castle that Wallace attempted to hold.

The short campaign in Annandale was over. Halliday settled down again in the Corhall and Kirkpatrick returned to Eskdale Wood. Wallace and Sir John, with 40 men, passed north into Lanarkshire, and having captured and dismantled Crawford Castle, proceeded straight to Dundaff.

The short and sharp campaigns of the west and the north – whether as detailed by Harry or not – had placed Wallace before his countrymen as the foremost champion of the liberties of Scotland.

CHAPTER IV

THE DELIVERANCE OF SCOTLAND

'Our power for to knaw,
We will tak feild, and wp our baner rais
Off rycht Scotland, in contrar off our fais.
We will no mar now ws in covert hid;
Power till ws will sembill on ilk syd.'

Harry, xi. 702–6

'The rycht is ouris, we suld mor ardent be;
I think to freith this land, or ellis de.'

Harry, ix. 821–2

'The Inglis men owt of owre land
He gert be put wyth stalwart hand.'

Wyntoun, viii. 13, 127–8

Leaving Dundaff, Wallace proceeded in April 1297 to Lanark, attended by nine men. He joined his wife in a house just outside the gate, and here Sir John the Graham came to him with fifteen followers. Sir William de Hazelrig[1], the Sheriff, the oppressor of his wife's family, and Sir Robert

---

[1] Bower calls him William de Heslope (Hislop). The indictment of Wallace has William de Hesebregg (Hazelrig); the b apparently a clerical blunder for l. Mr Joseph Bain (Cal. ii, p. 27) suggests Andrew de Livingstone, not convincingly. Livingstone preceded Hazelrig.

Thorn, presumably the Captain, soon devised a plan for taking him at disadvantage. As Wallace was returning from mass one May morning with his companions, not in armour but dressed in the civilian 'goodly green' of the season, he was ostentatiously insulted by an English soldier – 'the starkest man that Hazelrig then knew.' He tried to get away without a disturbance, but the arrival of Thorn and Hazelrig with some 200 men in harness at once precipitated a conflict. The odds were overwhelming, and the Scots retired through the gate, Wallace and Sir John doughtily defending the rear. Reaching Wallace's house, they were let in by his wife and passed out by a back door while she held the enemy in parley. They at once sought the shelter of Cartland Crags.

According to Harry, the English, enraged at being baffled, put Wallace's wife to death, but Harry professes himself unable to state the circumstances. Wyntoun, whose account is extremely similar to Harry's, says the Sheriff came to Lanark after the disturbance and then caused her to be put to death. He adds that Wallace secretly, but helplessly, witnessed her execution – an absolutely incredible assertion. Harry's version is certainly nearer the facts. The English had killed Wallace's father; they had persecuted his mother; now they had inhumanly murdered his wife. The cup was running over.

The distress of Wallace and his friends is finely depicted by Harry. It inflamed them to a desperate and exemplary revenge. Reinforced by Auchinleck with ten men, Wallace and his party entered Lanark at night by different gates in twos and threes without drawing attention to themselves. Wallace made for Hazelrig, Sir John for Thorn. Crashing in the door with his foot, Wallace found Hazelrig in his bedroom and slew him on the spot, while Auchinleck gave himself the satisfaction of 'making sikkar' with three thrusts of his knife. Young Hazelrig, rushing to the aid of his father, was also instantly slain. Meantime Sir John had burnt Thorn in his house.

Wallace drew off to Clydesdale for aid. His terrible wrongs and his signal revenge brought him troops of friends, and the hopes of patriotic Scotsmen rose high. Sir John the Graham and Auchinleck were at his side. Adam of Riccarton, Sir John of Tinto, Robert Boyd and Crawford (not Sir Reginald, who was in England) hastened to him. From Kyle and Cunningham came 1000 horsemen. Presently Wallace found himself at the head of 3000 'likely men of war', besides many footmen, who 'wanted horse and gear'.

One notable recruit deserves especial mention – Gilbert de Grimsby, whom Wallace's men rechristened Jop. Jop was a man 'of great stature' and already 'some part grey'. He was a Riccarton man by birth and had travelled far in Edward's service as 'a pursuivant in war', although, Harry says, he consistently refused to bear arms. No doubt he was the 'Gilbert de Grimmesby' who carried the sacred banner of St John of Beverley in Edward's progress through Scotland after Dunbar, a distinguished service for which Edward on 13 October 1296 directed Warenne to find him a living worth about twenty marks or pounds a year.

The news of the Lanark affray having reached Edward, Harry marches up to Biggar an 'awful host' of 60,000 men under the 'awful king' Edward and scatters it like husks of corn before Wallace, killing thousands, a fabulous number of the slain being near kinsmen of the king. But Edward was certainly in England at the time, busily struggling with adversity in his preparations 'to cross seas' to Flanders. He had, indeed, one eye on the Scots. In the beginning of May he was having his 'engines' – his military equipment – overhauled at Carlisle; on 24 May he addressed a circular order to his leading liegemen in Scotland to hear personally from certain high officers of 'certain matters he had much at heart' in view of his intended departure to Flanders; and through May and June he received the oaths of several Scots barons to serve him 'in Scotland against the king of France.' But, so far as authentic documents show, those preparations led elsewhere, not to Biggar. As there exists no historical record of this Biggar expedition and the local tradition is most likely a mere echo of Harry's trumpet, the Marquess of Bute and Dr Moir may be right in the suggestion that Harry's battle of Biggar is a duplicate of the later battle of Roslin. In any case, it must be seriously modified both in dimensions and in details.

Harry's account of Wallace's subsequent activities in the southwest must at present be left in a tangle of misconceptions. The dreadful story of the Barns of Ayr, however, claims notice. The details of the treacherous preparations must be rejected or at least held in grave suspense. The alleged result was that some 360 of the leading Scots of the district – Sir Reginald Crawford, Sir Bruce Blair, Sir Niel Montgomery, Crawfords, Kennedys, Campbells, Barclays, Boyds, Stewarts, and so forth – being summoned to attend a circuit court at Ayr on 18 June were hanged as they entered, one by one, in the 'Barns', or barracks, where the meeting was convened. Wallace, who had been specially aimed at, escaped by an accident.

Gathering what men he could muster on the spur of the

moment – some 300 – he came to the Barns at night, fired them and burnt and slew all the English there. Next he took the castle, but there were only a handful of men in it. Supplementary to the revenge taken by Wallace was 'the Friars' Blessing of Ayr'; for Friar Drumlay, the Prior, who had 140 English quartered with him, simultaneously rose with seven of his brethren, donned harness, and took arms and slew most of his guests, the few that escaped being drowned. Harry reckons the total slaughter at 5000.

What may be the kernel or fragments of truth in the story cannot now be stated. Certainly Sir Reginald Crawford was alive after 18 June. Arnulf the Justice may, as the Marquess of Bute suggests, stand for Ormsby the Justiciar, who was attacked by Wallace at Scone. The Marquess looks for explanation to the occasion of Edward's visit to Ayr on 26 August 1298, when the English found Ayr Castle burnt and abandoned. Lord Hailes supposes the story may have taken origin in the pillaging of the English quarters at Irvine in July 1297. Possibly there is a jumble and an exaggeration and distortion of all these facts, but there must be something deeper. The event is mentioned as well known, not only by Harry, but also by Barbour and Major and in the *Complaynt of Scotland*. The story as it stands does not fit into the known history of the time and place alleged and must be reserved for more adequate examination.

Wallace, according to Harry, proceeded straight to Glasgow, fearing that Bek and Percy might be perpetrating a similar atrocity at the court of justice they were holding for Clydesdale. He defeated the English in a stiff combat, killing Percy quite unhistorically. Bishop Bek, with an escort, escaped to Bothwell whither Wallace pursued him, but apparently he could not take him out of the hands of Sir Aymer de Valence. Bek was no doubt in Scotland somewhere about this time – perhaps two or three months later than Harry supposes, for Edward had sent him to report personally on the state of affairs concerning which various unwelcome indications had reached him.

One especially unwelcome report that the chroniclers specify as the immediate reason for dispatching Bek informed the king of a daring attack upon Ormsby, his Justiciar, at Scone by Wallace and Douglas. Ormsby demanded homage and fealty and punished non-performance with the utmost severity. 'The temper of Scotland at that season,' says Lord Hailes, 'required vigilance, courage, liberality, and moderation in its rulers. The ministers of Edward displayed none of these qualities. While other objects of interest or ambition occupied his thoughts, the administration of his officers became more and more abhorred and feeble.' This is true of Ormsby and true generally. Ormsby, forewarned of the approach of Wallace, just managed to escape, leaving all his belongings to the spoilers. Wallace and Douglas, it is said, killed a great many Englishmen and laid siege to several castles, but the details are not available.

The date of the attack on Ormsby is given by the chroniclers as May, but the seriousness of the situation must have impressed Edward before then, for we have seen that by this time he was preparing for a 'Scottish war'. The insurrectionary feeling was certainly stirring all over the country, and not merely within the range of Wallace's known operations. About this time, or a little later, Macduff had made an ineffectual rising in Fife. On 1 August Warenne reports from Berwick that the Earl of Strathearn had captured Macduff and his two sons, and 'they shall receive their deserts when they arrive.' About this time, or very little later, Sir Alexander of Argyll was reported to have taken the Steward's castle of Glasrog and to have invaded the lands of Alexander of the Isles, a liegeman of Edward. Has this anything to do with the expedition that Harry sends Wallace on to Argyll for the rescue of Campbell of Lochawe from MacFadyen, whom Edward had made Lord of Argyll and Lorn? After giving over the pursuit of Bek, Wallace had retired to Dundaff where Duncan of Lorn found him and called for his aid. Wallace promptly responded to the call of his old friend, defeated MacFadyen, and established Campbell and Duncan in their lands. At Ardchattan many men rallied to his standard, including Sir John Ramsay of Auchterhouse who had long held out in Strathearn, and with them he proceeded to attack St Johnston. Whatever the inaccuracies in Harry's details, it is quite certain that there now was revolt against English supremacy in Argyll.

The chroniclers join Douglas with Wallace in the attack on Ormsby. Harry does not mention the episode at all, and if he confuses it with the Barns of Ayr, he does not mention Douglas as present. It may be supposed that Douglas had come south from Scone and was engaged on a separate enterprise. Harry first puts him in independent action at a much later – and impossible – period. He makes Douglas attack and capture Sanquhar Castle, whereupon the captain of Durisdeer raised the Enoch, Tibbermoor and Lochmaben, and besieged him in Sanquhar. Douglas, in distress, sent for aid to Wallace, then in the Lennox. May it be Argyll and not the Lennox? Or did Wallace go to the Lennox after driving Bek out of Glasgow? The event must have been about this time, if ever. At any rate, Wallace promptly relieved him, defeated the English at Dalswinton, slaying 500, and made Douglas keeper from Drumlanrig to Ayr. Be all this as it may, Edward on 12 June confiscated all Douglas's lands and goods in Essex and Northumberland, which seems to indicate that by that date he had learned that Douglas had forsworn his liege lord.

In Galloway, Edward had further trouble with the shifty Bruce of Carrick. When the disturbance took place at Scone, the Bishop of Carlisle, acting with Edward's other high officers in these parts, summoned Bruce to appear and exacted from him an oath that he would lend faithful aid to the king against the Scots. This may have had nothing whatever to do with the Scone attack but may have been simply a part in the regular preparations that were going on for the 'Scottish war'. Bruce is supposed to have made a display of his fidelity by the raid he soon made on the lands of Douglas, carrying off Douglas's wife and children to Annandale. It is, however, an obvious suggestion that this vicious foray was a counterblow for the burning of Turnberry Castle in the Biggar campaign, if Douglas was with Wallace in that enterprise, as, on Harry's story, he probably was. Such an interpretation of Bruce's action would tend to confirm Harry on the point and there was no clear need for Bruce to signal his fidelity in that particular fashion.

At the same time, Bruce may have done it in order to cover up the conspiracy he was hatching with the Bishop of Glasgow, the Steward and the Steward's brother John. When the scheme was ripe, Bruce attempted in vain to raise his father's men of Annandale but he was supported by his own men of Carrick. His party at once fell to burning and slaying, and the chroniclers specially mention the expulsion and humiliating treatment of the English ecclesiastics. If such expulsion was to further the execution of the edict of April 1296, held in abeyance by the English domination, that was but a very subordinate consideration. The popular view seems to have been that Bruce was aspiring to the throne. Probably enough, at any rate, he thought that he might lead the nobles to the success that was likely otherwise to crown Wallace. There is no trace of any direct personal connection of Wallace with this movement – no trace except a blunder of Rishanger's, who mentions both Wallace and Andrew de Moray, (?Thomas or Herbert de Morham), but Walter of Hemingburgh rightly gives Douglas in place of Wallace and omits Moray. Bruce, of course, could not have been expected to put himself under the leadership of a mere landless squire whose proper place he would have considered to be that of a henchman of his own – a squire, moreover, who consistently professed to act as the liegeman of King John. No, the rising most probably represents an independent attempt of Bruce's party suggested by Wallace's successes.

Burton is not unnaturally surprised to find Sir William Douglas in Bruce's party. It would be easier for the Douglas pride to bow to Bruce than to Wallace, and the raid on the Douglas estates might be held to cancel the burning of Turnberry or might otherwise receive a large atonement. In any case, there is barely room for doubt that Douglas eventually, if not from the first, cast in his lot with Bruce. The plot proved a complete fiasco. An English army was upon them. In the first days of June, Edward had appointed Percy and Clifford 'to arrest, imprison, and "justify" all disturbers of the peace in Scotland and their resetters.' Having at length, with great difficulty, raised an army of 300 mounted men-at-arms and 40,000 foot in England north of the Trent, Percy and Clifford entered Annandale early in July. Pushing on to Ayr, they learned that the Scots force was near Irvine. The Scots barons are represented as being at sixes and sevens, so selfishly at strife that Sir Richard de Lundy, who had never done homage to Edward, passed over to Percy in open disgust at their discord. At any rate, they had neither the men, the military capacity or the patriotic ardour to stand up against the English army. They at once sued for terms. On 7 July, at Irvine, Percy and Clifford received them to Edward's peace, provisionally promising them their lives, property and personal liberty but requiring hostages. Such a weak and cowardly collapse of the joint enterprise of half a dozen of the most powerful Scots nobles, the natural leaders of the nation, with young Bruce himself at their head, may suggest some measure of the courage, resource and patriotism of the youthful and obscure Wallace – especially if we look only two months ahead to the signal victory of Stirling.

The craven spirit of these barons is pilloried in the ignominious document recording their appeal to Warenne to support the convention with Percy. There they stated shamelessly that they had been afraid lest Edward's coming army should harry their lands and that they had been surely informed that the king would impress 'all the middle people of Scotland' for his war overseas. They had accordingly taken up arms in defence until they could protect themselves by treaty from such a grievance and dishonour. 'And therefore, when the English army entered within the land, they came to meet them, and had such a conference that all of them came to the peace and the fealty of our lord the

King.' Yet their disgraceful treaty, negotiated by the Bishop of Glasgow, acknowledges that they had committed 'acts of arson, slaughter, and plunder'. They had to put the best face on a weak case. More spirit was shown by the nameless Scots and Glaswegians who plundered the English baggage in Irvine, slaying over 500 of the enemy while their betters were grovelling to Percy and Clifford for admission to the peace of the usurper.

On 15 July Percy and Clifford reached Roxburgh, where they found Cressingham with 300 covered horses and 10,000 foot soldiers, ready to march to their aid next morning. Cressingham's report to the king on 23 July throws interesting sidelights on the situation. Percy and Clifford appear to have thought that the whole object of the expedition had been accomplished. Cressingham, however, urged that 'even though peace had been made on this side the Scots water, yet it would be well to make a chevachie [raid] on the enemies on the other side,' or, at any rate, 'that an attack should be made upon William Wallace, who lay then with a large company – and does so still – in the Forest of Selkirk, like one that holds himself against your peace.' We shall presently see that the Scots north of Forth were tolerably active. Meantime Cressingham's reference to Wallace, as well as the formal treaty, appears to indicate all but conclusively that Wallace was no partner of the barons in the fiasco of Irvine. In the event, Percy and Cressingham decided to make no expedition until Warenne should arrive from England.

The next day both Cressingham and Spaldington wrote further particulars to Edward. Spaldington informed him that 'because Sir William Douglas has not kept the covenants he made with Sir Henry de Percy' – that is, had failed to provide hostages or guarantors – 'he is in your castle of Berwick, in my keeping, and he is still very savage and very abusive; but,' he added with dutiful zest, 'I will keep him in such wise that, please God, he shall by no means get out.'

Douglas was put in irons. On 12 October he was consigned to the Tower of London, and on 20 January 1299 he is reported as 'with God'. Again, Cressingham's letter of 24 July shows the irksomeness of the English position. Edward who had met almost insuperable difficulties in fitting out his Flanders expedition, had urged him to raise money from the issues and the rents of the realm of Scotland to aid Warenne and Percy in their military operations. 'Not a penny could be raised,' says Cressingham, 'until my lord the Earl of Warenne shall enter into your land and compel the people by force and sentence of law.' More than that:

'Sire, let it not displease you, by far the greater part of your counties of the realm of Scotland are still unprovided with keepers, as well by death, sieges, or imprisonment; and some have given up their bailiwicks, and others neither will nor dare return; and in some counties the Scots have established and placed bailiffs and ministers, so that no county is in proper order, excepting Berwick and Roxburgh, and this only lately.'

After all, Harry may not be far wrong in stating that Wallace appointed sheriffs and captains from 'Gamlispath' to Urr Water, and controlled Galloway after the alleged battle of Biggar. It may be also, as he says, that Douglas came to Wallace's peace at that time and ruled from Drumlanrig to Ayr as his lieutenant. In any case, Cressingham's letter mark emphatically the strength of the silent, as well as of the active, resistance of the people of Scotland. The impecunious and helpless Treasurer could qualify his rueful report by only one vague crumb of comfort. 'But, sire, all this will be speedily amended, by the grace of God, by the arrival of the said lord the Earl, Sir Henry de Percy, and Sir Robert Clifford, and the others of your Council.'

The alleged delay of the barons in giving hostages is attributed by the more trusted chroniclers to the urgency of Wallace. First Douglas, and then the bishop, surrendered their liberty, pricked (it is said) by insulting suspicions of their honour. But this seems to be matter of inference, not of fact. For on 1 August Warenne wrote to Edward: 'Sir William de Douglas is in your castle of Berwick, in good irons and in good keeping, for that he failed to produce his hostages on the day appointed him, as the others did.' As for the bishop, Edward's own theory, based (he said) on intercepted correspondence of Wishart, was that he had voluntarily submitted to internment in Roxburgh Castle in order to plot for its betrayal to the Scots. One would like to see that correspondence. No doubt the compulsion in both cases was altogether external.

At any rate, we are told that Wallace was extremely angry when he heard of their surrender and that, in his rage, he harried the bishop's house, carrying off his furniture, arms and horses. Possibly he did; possibly, too, the true story may be that this was the harrying of Bishop Bek, not of Bishop Wishart in Glasgow. It is further admitted that his followers increased to an immense number, the community of the land following him as their leader and chief, and the whole of the retainers of the magnates adhering to him; 'and although the magnates themselves were with our King in the body, yet their heart was far from him.' This picture agrees fully with the lamentable report of Cressingham.

The trouble in the north was certainly not to be ignored, as Cressingham well knew. Andrew de Moray, son of Sir Andrew de Moray (since Dunbar a prisoner in the Tower), was at the head of an insurrection of considerable size. The Bishop of Aberdeen and Gartnet, the son of the Earl of Mar, had proceeded to quell it, and early in June Edward had dispatched to their aid the Earl of Buchan and later the Earl of Mar. Mar, Comyn and Gartnet reported on 25 July that on 17 July at Launoy on the Spey 'met us Andrew de Moray with a great body of rogues,' and 'the aforesaid rogues betook themselves into a very great stronghold of bog and wood, where no horseman could be of service.' They mention 'the great damage which is in the country,' and send Sir Andrew de Rathe to inform him particularly. It is instructive to observe that, when Sir Andrew showed his credence to Cressingham at Berwick, Cressingham warned Edward (5 August) to give little weight to it, for it 'is false in many points, and obscure, as will be well known hereafter, I fear.' On the same date the Constable of Urquhart reported how Moray had besieged his castle, and about the same time Sir Reginald le Cheyne informed Edward how Moray and his 'malefactors' had spoiled and laid waste his goods and lands.

Apparently a peace had been patched up somehow, for on 28 August letters of safe-conduct were issued in favour of Andrew de Moray and of Hugh, son of the Earl of Ross, whose Countess had brought material aid to the English party against Andrew de Moray to enable both men to visit their fathers in the Tower of London. Andrew de Moray, however, could not have used his safe-conduct, for he fought at Stirling Bridge. By this time Aberdeen was also in revolt. On 1 August Warenne reports that 'we have sent to take Sir Henry de Lazom, who is in your castle of Aberdeen, and there makes a great lord of himself.' Warenne has not yet heard of Lazom's fate, but he can promise that 'if he be caught he shall be honoured according to his deserts.'

Wallace, whatever his strength in Selkirk Forest, evidently felt it inexpedient to offer direct opposition to the troops under Percy and Cressingham at Roxburgh and under Spaldington at Berwick. He went north, no doubt by Glasgow, if it is true that it was now he harried the facile bishop – or the astute one either. His force augmented steadily as he marched onward. It may have been at this time that he made the expedition into Argyll and Lorn; it may have been at the earlier date previously mentioned.

For some little space we must again fall back on the guidance of Harry, who, as we have just seen, brings him from Ardchattan to the siege of St Johnston. The details that Harry supplies give an air of truth and reality to his narrative. He tells how Sir John Ramsay had 'bestials' (towers used in sieges) of wood made in the forest and floated them down the river; how the troops filled the dykes with earth and stone and advanced the bestials to the walls; and how Wallace, Ramsay and Graham at last sacked the town, slaying 2000. Ruthven, who had joined with thirty men and distinguished himself in the siege, Wallace installed as Captain and Sheriff, with the hereditary lieutenancy of Strathearn.

'Then to the north good Wallace made him boun.'

Having first made a flying visit to Cupar, whence the English abbot had fled, Wallace swept over the north country with his accustomed energy. At Glamis he was joined by Bishop Sinclair; Brechin was reached the same night. The next morning Wallace displayed 'the banner of Scotland' and rode through the Mearns 'in plain battle' to Dunnottar Castle where some 4000 English had taken refuge. He destroyed them all, even burning down the church, which was full of refugees. Not even the intercession of the bishop could save them, for Wallace had fresh on his mind the atrocities of the Barns of Ayr.

Hastening to Aberdeen, Wallace suddenly came upon the shipping and destroyed it. Harry mentions no difficulty with the garrison. Wallace at once swept through Buchan and then round the farther north. It is impossible to say how the tour was affected by the results of the recent operations of Andrew de Moray west of the Spey. On 1 August – a rather early date – Wallace was back in Aberdeen making arrangements for the administration of the north. He immediately passed south to the siege of Dundee.

There are some historical blunders in Harry's sketch of Wallace's northern expedition. Sinclair, although a good patriot, was not Bishop of Dunkeld until 1308, at any rate not 'with the Pope's consent'; Matthew de Crambeth was bishop from 1288 to 1304 at least. Sir Henry de Beaumont too, whom Harry drives out of Buchan, was not earl until some ten years later. Again, if Wallace was in Selkirk Forest on 23 July, as Cressingham reported, he could not, with all his swiftness, have overrun the north and been back in Aberdeen by 1 August. It does not, however, by any means follow that Harry's account is not fairly right in substance. In any case, it seems certain that the whole of Scotland north of the

Forth – except Dundee and Stirling – was under the sway of Wallace just before the battle of Stirling Bridge.

On 22 August Edward embarked for Flanders and did not return to England until 14 March. A few days before sailing (14 August), he had designated Sir Brian Fitz Alan to succeed Warenne as Governor of Scotland, Warenne being ill and anxious to be relieved. In obedience to urgent orders to remain at his post, however, Warenne had gone north at the head of the English army and was making for Stirling. On hearing of his approach, Wallace left one of his lieutenants to carry on the siege of Dundee and hastened to dispute the passage of the Forth. He could not occupy Stirling Castle, for the castle was not, as Harry says, in the hands of Earl Malcolm (who, on the contrary, was in the English camp) but had been in the hands of Sir Richard de Waldegrave, the English Constable, since 8 September 1296.

Wallace chose his position with the instinct of military genius. With his back to the Abbey Craig and the Ochils above the Abbey of Cambuskenneth, and with a loop of the Forth protecting him in front, he commanded the head of the bridge that lay between him and the enemy. He is said to have had 180 horse and 40,000 foot, while Warenne had 1000 horse and 50,000 foot, but little reliance can be placed on the figures. Cressingham, it is said, had directed Percy to disband his army of the west, believing that the force under Warenne was amply sufficient for the campaign.

As the armies lay in view of each other, with the river rolling between them, negotiations took place with a view to some accommodation. The Steward of Scotland and Earl Malcolm of the Lennox readily obtained Warenne's permission to try what they could do in representations to Wallace.

Wallace, however, was absolutely irreconcilable. Warenne next dispatched two friars to Wallace to invite him and his men to come to the king's peace, promising impunity for all past offences. 'Take back for answer,' said Wallace, 'that we are not here to sue for peace, but are ready to fight for the freedom of ourselves and of our country. Let the English come on when they please, they shall find us ready to meet them to their beards.' The reply might have been anticipated.

In the English camp the report of the friars was correctly interpreted as a plain defiance and strengthened the clamour of Cressingham and his friends for an immediate attack on the presumptuous Scots. Warenne, ill and anxious to reach an easy settlement, was unable to withstand 'the ignorant impetuosity' of the overbearing churchman. Sir Richard de Lundy, whom Harry mistakenly ranges on the side of Wallace, interposed with a wise suggestion. He pointed out the fatal folly of attempting to advance over the bridge, which allowed only two to pass abreast; by that way 'we are dead men.' He offered to take a party of 500 horse and a detachment of infantry across a ford – 'probably the ford of Maner,' Hailes thinks – and catch the enemy in the rear. Lundy's proposal was declined on the flimsy ground that it would divide the army, the real ground probably being doubt of his fidelity. Still Warenne hesitated.

'Why do we drag out the war in this fashion,' urged the Treasurer, 'and waste the King's treasure? Let us fight, as is our bounden duty.' Warenne at last gave way.

On the morning of 11 September Cressingham led the English across the narrow bridge of Stirling. From the slopes of the Abbey Craig – over which now towers the imposing National Monument – Wallace sternly watched their column all morning until eleven o'clock. At the critical moment he sent the blast of his horn thrilling through the valley, the signal to launch his eager men upon the English. While the main bodies of the combatants met, a company of Scots seized and held the head of the bridge. This movement was no sooner realized than it embarrassed and disordered the advancing English and struck apprehension into the hearts of those who had passed over it. Hopeless confusion passed into irretrievable disaster. The English vanguard was cut to pieces or driven into the Forth. Cressingham himself was slain. Sir Marmaduke Twenge, who had been among the first to cross, seeing the inevitable rout, cut his way back to the bridge with conspicuous valour and made his escape. This remarkable exception indicates forcibly the plight of the rest. As the English drew back from the bridge, the Scots pressed vehemently upon them. Warenne, who had not crossed the river, promptly took to his horse and, ill as he was, did not stop until he reached Berwick and did not rest until he was safe on the English side of the Border.

It is said that the Scots flayed Cressingham's body and distributed the skin in strips. So deeply was he detested in life that it is far from unlikely that his enemies took a morbid revenge upon him in death. After all, it is only sentimentally worse than the fate he narrowly escaped at the hands of his own men, who were incensed almost to the point of stoning him to death for declining the aid of Percy's force.

The Steward and Earl Malcolm are represented as playing a double part, at which the Steward, at any rate, was getting well practised. Having failed to arrange an accommodation with Wallace, they had promised Warenne to bring him some 40 more horse on the day of battle. They discreetly waited to see how things would turn out and then calmly stood on the winning side with contemptible judiciousness.

The Scots at once set off in pursuit of Warenne's flying army. Harry traces the English flight through the Tor Wood, and on to Haddington and Dunbar. Wallace at once returned to Stirling. The constable of the castle, Sir Richard de Waldegrave, and a great part of the garrison had been killed at the bridge and Warenne had given the command to Sir William de Fitz Warin with whom was the redoubtable Sir Marmaduke de Twenge and 'other good soldiers'. The castle was quickly reduced 'from want of victuals'. Sir William de Ros, by his own account, was one of the captives and 'William le Waleys spared his life from being Sir Robert's brother (?cousin); but as he would not renounce his allegiance, sent him as a prisoner to Dumbarton Castle where he lay in irons and hunger till its surrender to the King after the battle of Falkirk.' On 7 April 1299, Edward authorized negotiations for the exchange of a number of prisoners, including Fitz Warin, Twenge and Ros. Fitz Warin died the same year (before 23 December). The fate of the rest of the garrison was probably similar.

Harry tells how Wallace received all the barons who were willing to come to him, requiring them all to swear 'a great oath' to be loyal to himself and to Scotland with the alternative of death or imprisonment. Sir John de Menteith he mentions specifically as having taken the oath. But this subordination of the 'barons' – in spirit at least – is to be accepted with some reserve, although an English annalist also tells us that the Scots adhered to Wallace 'from the least to the greatest', and the papers about 'ordinances and confederations' found on Wallace's person when he was captured, point to a pact of some sort. Dundee was at once evacuated; and in ten days not an English captain was left in Scotland except in Berwick and Roxburgh. Wallace had at length achieved the deliverance of Scotland.

CHAPTER V

WALLACE, GUARDIAN OF SCOTLAND

'Be caus I am a natyff Scottis man,
It is my dett to do all that I can
To fend our kynrik out off dangeryng.'
                    Harry, viii, 545–7
'The grettast lordis of oure land,
Til him he gert them be bowand.'
                    Wyntoun, viii, 13, 119–20
'Sa afald wes ay for the commoun weill.'
                    Boece, Cron. xlvii, 802

The immediate outcome of the victory of Stirling Bridge
was the clearance of the English out of the realm of Scotland. At the same time, the success gave no measure of the
relative strength of the two countries, now fully transformed
from friendly neighbours into bitter enemies. It in no way
diminishes the glory of Wallace to recognize the accidental
weakness of the English at Stirling – the illness of Warenne,
the headstrong folly of Cressingham and the absence of
Edward in Flanders. Wallace, on the other hand, had also his
own disadvantages in men and means, owing especially to
the fatal operation of the feudal machinery of society. He

was grievously weakened by the absence of adherents of hereditary name and territorial importance, and yet the presence of such adherents was soon destined to paralyse his efforts. Whatever the difficulties of Edward – foreign expeditions, vexatious claims of intractable barons or lack of ready money – he could always in the last resort raise a large army of veteran troops against which Wallace could not possibly hold an even field. But then Wallace had the courage never to submit or yield. The military determination of such a conflict could not lie in a single decisive battle; it could be reached only through long years of desultory and embittered warfare. Yet the victory of Stirling was all-important to the Scots in demonstrating that even the mighty armies of England might be disastrously overthrown and that Scotland might, after all, succeed in throwing off the intolerable yoke of foreign domination. It was a star of hope.

There can be little doubt as to the course taken by the Scots leaders after the expulsion of the English. They summoned a council or convention at St Johnston. At this council they elected William Wallace and Andrew de Moray 'generals of the army of Scotland', with full civil powers as well in the name of King John. By the victory of Stirling, Wallace stood forth the foremost man in Scotland. He had held the leadership and he had proved himself worthy. But while his rewards were beyond dispute, there was a natural reluctance on the part of the barons to serve under such a 'new man', and to obviate this difficulty, it was necessary, or at least desirable, to join with him in command a representative of the baronage.

The choice of Andrew de Moray was no doubt suggested by his conspicuous services, especially his recent action in

Moray and his conduct at the bridge. Baronial considerations may also explain the official precedence of Moray's name. Some of the chroniclers say that Sir Andrew de Moray, his father, fell at Stirling, but Sir Andrew was lying safe in the Tower of London. The report of an inquisition at Berwick in 1300 incidentally mentions that it was Andrew de Moray himself who fell at Stirling, but this must be an error. The fallen Moray must have been some other member of the brave and prolific family of Morays.

For all practical purposes, at any rate, the interests of the country were in the keeping of Wallace, and he undoubtedly proceeded to establish order with a firm hand and with unflagging energy. One of the most powerful of the Scots nobles, Patrick Earl of March, did not appear to the summons to council. The general feeling, Harry tells us, ran in favour of proceeding against him without delay. Wallace, however, deprecated such brusqueness of action and induced the council to dispatch a special invitation to the earl urging him to come and take his proper place in the counsels of his countrymen. Patrick, however, returned an insulting answer, contemptuously pointed at Wallace, whom he called a 'King of Kyle', implying thereby much what Langtoft means when he calls Wallace a 'master of thieves', for Kyle signifies 'forest' as well as designates the district of Wallace's birth. Thereupon Wallace at once went against him, defeated him in a hard fight near Dunbar and took his castle, Patrick himself escaping into England. Even after the expedition into England, which was no doubt now resolved upon, had reached Berwick, Wallace, it is said, on learning that certain recalcitrants as far north as Aberdeen ignored the summons to provide aid, left Moray in charge and proceeded at once to the spot, where he promptly hanged those who failed to offer a good excuse. Wallace appears to have carried out consistently the rule of driving from Scotland every Englishman, layman or ecclesiastic with the exception of the garrison of Roxburgh. Scotland for the Scots! On the death of Fraser, he had William de Lamberton appointed Bishop of St Andrews, defeating the opposition of William Comyn, brother of the Earl of Buchan.

The military situation was but a temporary respite and required instant preparation for both attack and defence. The condition of the country was lamentable. The land south of the Forth had been denuded of everything likely to afford subsistence to the invaders, and what the Scots had not drawn off had been eaten up or destroyed by the English troops. Throughout Scotland there was severe scarcity, if not actual famine, with pestilence in its track. With the view of relieving the pressure at home and of adding to the supplies from the plenty of the northern counties of England, as well as of heartening his men and people by striking a counter-blow to the enemy in their own territory, Wallace – or the Council – projected a strong foray across the border. For that enterprise, however, it was necessary to make adequate preparations.

Wallace appears not to have remained content with marshalling afresh his Stirling forces with the later recruits who flocked to his standard. He is stated to have now made a deliberate attack upon the feudal structure that hampered him so menacingly. He is said to have divided the country into military districts, establishing district muster rolls of all persons between sixteen and sixty capable of bearing arms. Over every four men he appointed a fifth; over every nine, a tenth; over every nineteen, a twentieth; and so on upwards. A gibbet frowning over every parish enforced respect to the conscription; examples were not lacking. The barons were threatened with imprisonment or confiscation in case they offered any obstacle to the incorporation of their vassals in the army of liberation. The particular process outlined by the later historian Bower may be no more than his own interpretation of facts he little understood, but there need be no hesitation in believing that Wallace at this time made some strenuous effort of reorganization directed to blunting the force of feudal influences as well as to rendering his army both more flexible and more efficient.

At the same time it is certain that his mind was much occupied in devising means of alleviating the internal distress caused by the prolonged inflictions of foreign invasion and foreign occupation. The trading activity of the seaports, animated by settlers from the Continent, notably by enterprising Flemings, had permeated and revived the whole country, but the wars had seriously checked the streams of business across the North Sea as well as the inland trade and industry. That Wallace took energetic measures to improve the situation was placed beyond question by Lappenberg's discovery (1829) of a most significant letter still extant in the archives of the city of Lübeck. This letter, in Latin, translates as follows:

'Andrew de Moray and William Wallace, the Generals of the army of the realm of Scotland, and the Community of the same realm, to the prudent and discreet men and well-beloved friends, the Mayors and Commons of Lübeck and Hamburg, greeting, and increase ever of sincere friendship.

'We have learned from trustworthy merchants of the said

realm of Scotland that you, of your own goodwill, lend your counsel, aid, and favour in all matters and transactions touching us and the said merchants, although we on our part have previously done nothing to deserve such good offices; and all the more on that account are we bound to tender you our thanks and to make a worthy return. To do so we willingly engage ourselves to you, requesting that you will make it known among your merchants that they can have safe access to all the ports of the realm of Scotland with their merchandise; for the realm of Scotland, thank God, has been recovered by war from the power of the English. Farewell.

'Given at Hadsington [Haddington], in Scotland on October 11, in the year of Grace 1297.

'We further request you to have the goodness to forward the business of John Burnet and John Frere, merchants of ours, as you would wish us to forward the business of merchants of yours. Farewell. Given as above.'

Moray and Wallace, it is to be noted, designate themselves 'the Generals' and join with themselves 'the Community' of Scotland. They are Joint Guardians in effect, although not in official name.

The Scots army mustered on Roslin Moor. As it approached the border, the English settlers in Roxburgh and Berwick mostly fled into Northumberland, whence the Northumbrians themselves were fleeing to the protection of Newcastle. Towards the end of October, the Scots streamed into England and ravaged Northumberland at will, molested only in its fringes by occasional minor resistance from strongholds like Alnwick Castle. Here they derived effective assistance from the local knowledge and strong arm of Sir Robert de Ros of Wark, and they apparently made Rothbury Forest a rallying ground. They next directed their

107

march to Carlisle, but Carlisle, like Alnwick, was too strongly fortified to yield to besiegers unprovided with 'engines' (siege equipment). We have the bishop's word for it, however, that they wasted the surrounding countryside, and the chroniclers tell us how they crossed Englewood Forest and Allerdale with fire and sword, penetrating as far as to the Derwent at Cockermouth. Crossing country again from Cumberland, with designs on the bishopric of Durham, they were repelled by a timely storm – hail, snow and hard frost – invoked by St Cuthbert. Many of them, Hemingburgh affirms, perished from hunger and cold. They fell back on Hexham.

At Hexham Priory, which Comyn's expedition had left in ruins some eighteen months before, the Scots found only three canons who had bravely ventured to return. They now took refuge in the oratory, that they had newly erected in the midst of the desolation, there to die, should such be the will of God, in the odour of holiness.

'Show us the treasury of your church,' roared the marauders, brandishing their spears, 'or you shall instantly die.'

'It is no long time,' stoutly replied one of the canons, 'since you and your people carried off pretty well everything we possessed, and what you have done with it you know best yourselves. Since then, we have got together but a few things, as you now see.'

At this moment, Wallace himself opportunely entered, and ordering his men to fall back, requested that one of the canons would celebrate mass. On the elevation of the Host, Wallace went out to lay aside his arms and, when he was about to receive the sacred elements, the Scots crowded up to him with the intention of snatching away the chalice. He withdrew into the sacristy to wash his hands. Then the greed of the soldiers broke loose. They seized the chalice from the altar where the canon had left it in unsuspecting confidence, the napkins, the altar ornaments and the very mass book the canon had been using. Wallace, on his return, found the canon in bewildered consternation and instantly ordered the culprits to be sought for and beheaded. They were not found, says the historian ruefully, 'for the seeking was without intention of finding.' Wallace, however, took the canons under his immediate protection, warning them to keep close to him, for his men recognized neither law nor punishment.

This story, Canon Raine thinks, 'was probably told to the historian by his brother canon, William de Hexham, who migrated from the north to Leicester in 1321.' Knighton of Leicester, however, copied or adapted the story from Hemingburgh, but Hemingburgh himself may have got it at Guisborough in Yorkshire in some such direct way. It forms a very striking episode, and it fits in perfectly with Wallace's grant of two charters – one of protection and one of safe-conduct – to the prior and convent.

The violence of the soldiery of the time, Scots or English, is a fact, demanding such blame or excuse as may be fairly evoked by the circumstances of each case. The specific protections now issued by Wallace, as certified by Hemingburgh, himself an English chronicler, constitute a conspicuous testimony to the hero's humanity. Did Wallace's conduct touch the old chronicler himself? In this story he drops his usual epithet for Wallace – 'that notorious bandit' (*ille latro*). We refrain from pressing the obvious contrasts to Wallace's considerate action. The charter of protection to the prior and convent of Hexham may be rendered thus:

'Andrew de Moray and William Wallace, Generals of the army of Scotland, in the name of the renowned Prince Lord John, by the grace of God, the illustrious King of Scotland, with the consent of the Community of the same realm, to all men of the said realm to whom the present writing shall come, greeting, –

'Know that we, in the name of the said King, have duly taken the Prior and convent of Hexham in Northumberland, their lands, their men, and the whole of their possessions, including all their goods, movable and immovable, under the firm peace and protection of the said Lord King and of ourselves. Wherefore we strictly forbid that any one presume to do them any evil, annoyance, injury, or offence in their persons, lands, or goods, under penalty of forfeiture of all the offender's property to the said Lord King, or to put them, or any one of them, to death, under penalty of loss of life and limbs. These presents to remain in force for one year and no longer.

'Given at Hexham, November 7.'

A letter of safe-conduct was at the same time granted in the following terms:

'Andrew de Moray and William Wallace . . . (as before)

'Know that we have received one canon of Hexham, with his squire and two attendants, to the safe and secure conduct of our King and of ourselves, to enable them to come to us wherever we may be, whenever it shall be necessary and expedient for the said house. And therefore, in the name of the said Lord King, we order and strictly enjoin you, all and every, that, when any canon of the said house, with the squire aforesaid and his attendants, shall come to you with the object of coming to us, bearing the present letter, you conduct them to us under safe charge, in such manner that no one shall molest them in their persons or in their belongings in any respect, under penalty of forfeiture of all the offender's property to the King, or shall put them or any of them to death, under penalty of loss of life and limbs. These presents to remain in force during our pleasure.'

Moray and Wallace are still 'the Generals of the army of Scotland', but now it is further stated that they are acting in the name of King John. The deposition of John is defiantly ignored. It has been supposed that between 11 October and 7 November John had sent them a commission authorizing them to act under his sanction. This is not impossible, but the step would have involved extreme risk of personal danger to himself however it might have strengthened the official influence of the Generals. It seems too hazardous to conjecture that the fresh expression implies a fresh sanction, obtained in such circumstances. One had rather regard it as simply a fuller statement of the view that the Generals now, if not all along, held as to the nature of their position. There seems little reason, however, to doubt that the Council had from the first resolved that all official acts should be in the name of King John.

Having spent two days at Hexham, the expedition headed for Newcastle, burning Ritton on the way The garrison of Newcastle showed fight, and the garrison of Durham also; otherwise there was no opposition. The Scots had no means to enter upon an effective siege and, accordingly, they wasted no efforts upon an attempt. They recrossed the border about Christmas, having had their way in the three northern counties for the best part of two months.

The narratives of the incursions are, perhaps unavoidably, somewhat confused. The movements of the Scots seem to have been exceedingly rapid. They may, not improbably, have come and gone in relays, keeping temporary headquarters in Rothbury Forest, and it may be that the incidents are not all treated in their right order. But the general account of a comprehensive ravage of the three northern counties from Tweed to Tyne and Derwent during November and December is solid fact. The effects of the visitation may be partly gathered from Hemingburgh's narrative. 'During that time,' he says 'the praise of God ceased in all the monasteries and churches of the whole province from Newcastle-upon-Tyne to Carlisle; for all the monks, canons regular, and other priests, servants of the Lord, had fled, with (one may say) the whole of the common folk, from the face of the Scots.' We cannot attend Harry on his rambles to two sieges of York and a descent upon St Albans (to say nothing of the queen's embassy); much less can we go with Boece as far as Kent – which his editor, however, boldly converts into 'Tyne'.

About the same time, Sir Robert de Clifford, the Warden of the Western Marches, had executed a diversion by way of reprisal. He sallied from Carlisle with 110 men-at-arms and (says Hemingburgh) 20,000 chosen foot soldiers, crossed the Solway and ravaged Annandale with fire and sword, carrying back considerable booty. The raiders returned to Carlisle on Christmas Eve. Probably Clifford had in fact no great force at his command even if the levies ordered for him in Lancashire in the middle of November had by this time joined him. Towards the end of February he made a similar foray and burnt the town of Annan, but apparently this was a less forcible effort than the raid of December.

Meantime, extensive preparations had been in progress in England for a fresh expedition against the Scots. Edward was still in Flanders. After Stirling Bridge Warenne had gone to consult with Prince Edward at York. On 24 September, the northern barons, who had been summoned to join the prince in London, were directed to join Warenne, and Clifford and Fitz Alan were instructed to act in concert with him. On 23 October Ormsby received orders to raise levies numbering over 35,000 men. On 26 October it was ordered that provisions and stores should be forwarded from all the eastern seaboard, by sea and land, to Holy Island or Newcastle. On 10 December an order was issued for levies to be raised in Wales and to be ready at Durham or Newcastle by 28 January at the latest. On the same day Warenne was formally appointed to the command. The available strength of England was to be hurled against Scotland.

The main body of the English army was to assemble at York on 20 January. On the 14th a parliament was held. The English magnates attended in great force, and their goodwill was conciliated by a confirmation of Magna Carta (with certain additional concessions) and of the Forest Charter, sent by Edward from Flanders. The Scots nobles who had been summoned 'neither came nor sent'.

Warenne proceeded to Newcastle. There, on 28 January, Hemingburgh says, he marshalled 2000 armed horse, over 1200 unarmed horse and more than 100,000 foot, including the Welsh contingent, and the army was steadily augmented as it advanced. Warenne relieved Roxburgh and recovered Berwick, the Scots having retired before his overwhelming force. There, however, his expedition was stopped by a dispatch from Edward announcing the conclusion of peace with France and directing Warenne to hold Berwick but not to undertake any enterprise of importance until he himself should arrive. Warenne therefore temporarily disbanded his army, retaining with him in Berwick 1500 armed horse and some 20,000 foot from Wales and from the remoter parts of England.

The retreat of the English before the Scots at Stanmore is very differently related by Scots and English historians, and the Scots writers are undoubtedly wrong in stating that Edward himself was present. It can be readily explained by the orders to Warenne, and, in any case, it is of no importance. Plainly the Scots were unable to hold the open field. How Wallace was engaged immediately after the retreat from Roxburgh, where he is said to have been personally in command, we do not know. It seems probable that, amidst all his concern for the military situation, he was not neglecting the internal reorganization of the country. On 29 March 1298, he granted to Alexander Scrymgeour the hereditary Constableship of Dundee 'for his faithful service and aid in bearing the Royal Banner in the army of Scotland', a service he was then actually performing. The charter bears to be granted by 'Sir William Wallace, Guardian of the realm of Scotland and leader of the armies of that realm, in the name of the renowned Prince Lord John, by the Grace of God, the illustrious King of Scotland, with the consent of the community of the said realm.' In the body of the document the grant is stated to be made 'by the consent and approbation of the magnates of the said realm.' 'The common seal of the aforesaid realm of Scotland' is stated to be impressed on the charter, and the seal of John is attached. The place of grant is Torphichen.

Andrew de Moray is no more in joint authority – very likely he had died – and Wallace is officially designated

'Guardian of the realm of Scotland'. He may, as is usually said, have been elected in the Forest of Selkirk – a very wide place in those days – and the immediate reason may possibly have been the expediency of an undivided authority in the face of an overwhelming army of invasion. Lord Hailes says he 'assumed' the title, but if this means that Wallace adopted the title without having it conferred on him, the suggestion is wholly improbable. It is interesting to know that on 5 December 1303 (?1300), Bruce, as one of the Guardians, recognized and enforced this charter.

It is a point of small importance when or by whom, if ever, Wallace was formally knighted, but since it has been made an occasion for carping at Wallace, we may quote from an English political song in the absence of better authority. Philip of France, in a letter quoted on a subsequent page, styles him *miles*, but the objectors say that may mean simply 'soldier'. The song says:

> 'Jam redit in Scotiam populus malignus;
> Et Willelmo datum est militare pignus;
> De praedone fit eques, ut de corvo cignu
> Accipit indignus sedem, cum non prope dignus.'

That is to say: 'Now return to Scotland the malignant people; and to William is given the knightly pledge – knighthood: from a robber he becomes a knight, as from a raven a swan; the unworthy takes the seat, when there is none worthy by.' Thanks to the 'malignant' poet. The writer of the Cottonian manuscript, referring to this song, states that it was one of the foremost Scots earls who girded Wallace with the belt of knighthood but he places the date just before, not after, the foray into England.

Edward landed at Sandwich on 14 March and lost no time in pushing forward the Scottish expedition. He accommodated his nobles with a promise of reconfirmation of the charters, the York confirmation not having been made in England. Fresh orders were issued for provisions, the Carlisle depot to be specially supplied from Ireland. A parliament was held at York on 25 May, the place and date originally fixed for the gathering. Again, it is stated, the Scots nobles summoned 'neither came nor sent'. On 27 May Edward issued orders to the sheriffs to have their men up at Roxburgh by 23 June, and the next day he appointed Earl Patrick Captain of Berwick Castle. Meantime he sought inspiration at the shrines of St John of Beverley and of two other less famous saints. On reaching Roxburgh, he found his army ready to march. According to Hemingburgh, there were 3000 armed horse, 4000 unarmed horse and 80,000 foot, consisting largely of Welsh and Irish. At the head of this immense force, Edward advanced to Kirkliston.

By this time Sir Aymer de Valence and Sir John Siward, who had sailed direct from Flanders, had landed in Fife. Wallace found them in the Forest of Blackearnside and defeated them severely on 12 June. He is said to have lost Sir Duncan Balfour, Sheriff of Fife, and perhaps Sir Christopher Seton, while Sir John the Graham was badly wounded. This is one of Blind Harry's great fights. One would much like to have certain authority for his statement that Wallace, in a respite from actual fighting in the heat of the day, instead of taking much needed rest, carried water in a helmet from a neighbouring brook for the relief of his wounded men. We should not hesitate to accept it, on a general impression of the character and temperament of the Guardian. Having reasserted his authority in Fife, Wallace drew south again to keep the English army under observation.

The English army lay at Kirkliston. Edward had suffered much annoyance from parties sallying on the fringes of his army from Dirleton and two other castles, and he had sent the Bishop of Durham to reduce them. The bishop found his task by no means an easy one. He was not well furnished either with provisions or with equipment, and the garrison of Dirleton fought him manfully. He sent a messenger to Edward, a truculent soldier, Sir John Fitz Marmaduke. With a subhumorous reply to Antony, Edward is said by Hemingburgh to have thus instructed Fitz Marmaduke: 'You are a relentless soldier, Marmaduke. I have often had to reprove you for too cruel exultation over the death of your enemies. But return now whence you came, and be as relentless as you choose – you will deserve my thanks, not my censure. But look you do not see my face again till these three castles are razed to the ground.' The three castles were soon taken and burnt down.

Still Edward waited anxiously for his provision ships from Berwick, which had been long detained by winds. There was little to be got from the country around, for the Scots had adopted the usual tactics and cleared the land before the approach of the enemy. The army began to feel the sharp pinch of hunger. The Scots, perfectly aware of the plight of the English, were keeping close in touch with them, ready to harass the anticipated retreat. At last some provisions arrived, including 200 casks of wine, which Edward did not hesitate to distribute freely. Two of the casks, it is stated, went to the Welsh who had broken down greatly, many of them having died. Some of the Welshmen got drunk, raised

117

a quarrel with some of the English, and eventually a fight developed, killing eighteen English ecclesiastics, possibly peacemakers, and wounding many more. A party of English horse, excited by the disturbance, charged upon the Welsh, and killed eighty of them, the rest taking to flight. If, as Hemingburgh says, there were 40,000 Welsh – or even, as another writer says, 10,000 – the two casks look like a meagre proportion monopolized by a few.

The whole of the Welsh contingent stood aloof, and it was believed in the English camp that they would go over to the Scots unless some steps were taken to placate them. Edward, relying no doubt on his mounted troops, treated the camp rumours with contempt:

'What matter if enemies join with enemies? Let them go where they please; we will beat the Scots and them too.'

But still the gripe of hunger tightened upon his men, and it must have been a cruel moment for him when at last he gave the order to prepare to retire to Edinburgh.

Suddenly, however, the order was reversed, much to the astonishment of the camp. Early in the morning of 21 July the king had learned that the Scots army was not far away, near Falkirk, in the Forest. He at once put his men under arms and moved steadily forward to seek the enemy. That night the English encamped some way east of Linlithgow, lying on their arms in the fields. The horses had nothing to eat – 'nothing but hard iron' – and were kept in readiness beside their riders. On this occasion Edward himself met with an awkward accident attributed to a page's lack of care. His mount trampled on him as he lay asleep, says Hemingburgh, and as news of his hurt passed through the army, there arose shouts of treason and exclamations that the enemy were on them. According to Rishanger, there broke out a terrible uproar in the camp at daybreak, under the impression that the enemy were at hand, and the king's steed, catching the excitement, threw him as he mounted and kicked him in the side, breaking two ribs. Both accounts testify to a lively sense of insecurity in the English camp. Edward, with the stoical firmness of a veteran, mounted another horse and advanced with his army.

As day broke on 22 July, Edward passed Linlithgow. With the growing light, he discovered the Scots ready for battle. Wallace now lacked the natural strength of the slopes of the Abbey Craig, but he again showed his military ability by a masterly disposition of his troops – masterly, yet desperately daring. The real strength of the Scots cannot be even approximately estimated, but although one English chronicler mentions that prisoners said there were 300,000 foot, and another English scribe numbers them at over 200,000, and yet another imaginative English annalist says 100,000 of them were slain, it is extremely unlikely that they approached the numbers of the English.

Be this as it may, Wallace threw the whole of his infantry in front, arranging them in four circular bodies, or schiltrons, to receive cavalry, the front rank sitting on their heels, the next ranks successively rising and all presenting to the enemy an oblique 'wood of spears'. The intermediate spaces were occupied by the archers under the command of Sir John Stewart of Bonkill, the Steward's brother. The cavalry were placed in the rear: even the English chroniclers do not number these higher than 1000. The front of the position was protected by a peat moss, or turf bog, and it was further strengthened by a stockade consisting of long stakes firmly driven into the ground and connected securely by ropes. On the military theory of the day, which laid all stress on iron-clad horse and relegated footmen to contemptuous subordination, the Scots were hopelessly inferior. It may safely be said that no competent living general except Wallace would have dared to meet Edward in the open field on such terms, and it seems all but certain that even Wallace would not have dared it otherwise than as a desperate alternative to an impossible retreat. The dispositions completed, Wallace is said to have addressed his first line in one of his crisp, bright and homely speeches: 'I have brought you to the ring: hop [dance] if you can.' The remark glows with the joy of battle and thrills with the general's confidence in the prowess of his men.

On the English side, there is no record of the dispositions of the infantry – a comparatively unconsidered quantity. The cavalry was massed in two main divisions: the first under the Earl Marshal and the Earls of Hereford and Lincoln; the second under the warlike Bishop of Durham and Sir Ralph Basset of Drayton. The rest of the army, horse and foot, was immediately under the king himself.

Edward opened the attack by ordering the Welsh to advance, no doubt making a preliminary trial of their temper. The Welsh, however, 'from the inveterate hatred they bore the King' (says Rishanger), declined to move, possibly with an idea of joining eventually the side that should prove victorious. Edward accordingly gave the signal to the first cavalry division. The Earl Marshal rode straight ahead, ignorant of the peat bog in front, but after a little embarrassment, he led his men round the west side and dashed upon the Scots right. The bishop was before him, however, having known of the bog, and having led his men round the east end had already struck the left of the foremost Scots circles. The hedge of stakes had gone down with a crash. The Scots cavalry, witnessing the combined shock of the English horsemen, fled without striking a blow. The bowmen were the next to fail, although not with dishonour. Their commander, Sir John Stewart, fell from his horse while directing the operations of the Selkirk Forest contingent and was killed in the thickest of the onset. His men – fine tall men, says Hemingburgh – bravely although vainly, formed around him and fell by his side. The spearmen, however,

> 'still made good
> Their dark impenetrable wood,
> Each stepping where his comrade stood,
> The instant that he fell.'

The defence was undoubtedly magnificent. The cavalry could neither break up the circles nor ride them down. At last a large body of infantry was brought up, armed partly with arrows, partly with stones, which harassed the Scots and eventually disorganized the front line. The moment the edge of the schiltron showed a gap, the cavalry dashed in and the battle was converted into a massacre.

The Scots losses must have been very heavy: one annalist runs them up to 'about' 100,000 – 'like snow in winter' – 'the living could not bury the dead'. Hemingburgh is content with 50,000 foot slain, besides some 30 horsemen and an unknown number drowned. Sir John Stewart and his men of Bute and Macduff and his men of Fife died where they stood. Sir John the Graham is also said to have fallen:

Wallace's lament over his dead body forms one of the finest passages in Harry's poem. The most distinctive loss on the English side was Sir Brian le Jay, the Master of the Templars in England. The English loss in common folk cannot even be guessed at: one patriotic scribe places it at 'about 30 foot'.

Lord Hailes remarks on 'the fatal precipitancy of the Scots'. 'If,' he says, 'they had studied to protract the campaign, instead of hazarding a general action at Falkirk, they would have foiled the whole power of Edward, and reduced him to the necessity of an inglorious retreat.' But there surely can be no question that this was the very policy of Wallace, now as ever, and we have seen how very near Edward was to a retreat upon Edinburgh, which must soon have been extended to a retreat into England. If this is so, the real question is, Why did the policy fail? The Scots were, of course, keeping as close to the English as was consistent with safety in order to take advantage of the opportunities offered by a retreat necessitated by hunger. Were they suddenly caught, so as to be unable to retire without excessive danger? The greater probability seems to be that they were, for it is inconsistent with Wallace's stern assertion of authority to believe that he would have yielded his better judgment to the urgency even of the Steward and Comyn. How did it come about, then, that a general of Wallace's discretion, vigilance and personal activity allowed himself to be caught?

The Scots chroniclers tell of grave and heated dissension among the Scots captains. Comyn is said to have worked on the pride of the Steward so as to induce him to claim to lead the vanguard. We can quite believe that Wallace, on hearing this claim offensively urged, 'burnt as fire', as Harry says he did. It was not, as Hailes jeeringly misrepresents, a question of 'the punctilio of leading the vanguard of an army which stood on the defensive.' The claim was simply an insolent usurpation of the plain function of the Guardian of Scotland – a claim, too, preferred by a noble whose conduct had aggravated Wallace's difficulties in making a Scots Guardian of Scotland so much as a possibility. Wallace's resentment was most just and proper; the absence of it would have been contemptible lack of courage, and it is impossible to doubt that Wallace would sooner have died on the spot, at the hands of the English or otherwise, than have submitted for a moment to any such pretension on the part of any man living, Balliol alone excepted. Nor is it at all in consonance with one's conception of the character of Wallace that he would, as Harry says he did, have stood apart under the constraint of a heated vow and let the Steward be borne down by the enemy: such a representation is no less degrading than preposterous. Boece is no authority, indeed, but it is interesting to remark that he explicitly denies Harry's version and says Wallace fought hard and was unable to help the Steward – a vastly more probable story. Whatever dissensions there may have been – and it is far from improbable that baronial pride did give rise even to violent dissensions – still such dissensions would, as Hailes remarks, have had no 'influence on their conduct in the day of battle.' But the proposition must be guarded by a proviso neglected by Hailes; and that essential proviso is that all the men were honest patriots. For the moment, there need be no question as to the temporary patriotism of the Steward.

It is different with Comyn. Comyn is believed, almost with certainty, to have commanded the cavalry, and the cavalry fled at the mere sight of the first shock on the schiltrons without striking a blow or even waiting to see what was to happen to the foot circles. Now, Hailes thinks the truth of the matter is this: that the Scots cavalry, seeing that they were greatly outnumbered by the English cavalry and far less effectively equipped, were intimidated and fled. But they knew all that before. Even if they had remained on the field, Hailes thinks, although they might have preserved their honour, they never could have turned the chance of the day. It was natural, he adds, for such of the infantry as survived to attribute their disaster to the defection of the cavalry; a natural pride would ascribe their flight to treachery rather than to lack of courage. Well, the readiness to invoke treachery as an explanation of such reverses is very familiar, but it does not follow that it is always untrue. It is impossible, however, to ascribe cowardice to Comyn personally, nor does Hailes do so, but it is equally impossible to attribute cowardice without proof to Comyn's men any more than to the humbler men of the schiltrons. This, however, is what Hailes quietly takes to be true, for he says the commander must follow his men, as Warenne did from Stirling Bridge, although he forgets that Warenne did not budge until it was plain to everybody that the day was disastrously lost. Comyn could not have been unaware of Wallace's expectations from the schiltrons, based on tried experience in many another, if smaller, combat. Whether or not his active assistance would have turned the day is unknown, but the stubborn resistance of the schiltrons shows that an additional force of 1000 horse would have proved very materially helpful. In any case, the very least Comyn could have done would have been to attempt to break the force of the attack on the schiltrons and, when the schiltrons were finally broken, to have protected the rear of the retreat, as no doubt Wallace himself did with a body of his devoted lieutenants. Lack of courage is no appropriate label for such glaring misconduct as Comyn's.

Hailes finds ample vindication of Comyn in the fact that he was presently chosen one of the Guardians in succession to Wallace. It is said that Sir John Comyn was made Guardian on Wallace's resignation and that Sir John de Soulis was associated with Comyn by Balliol. If so, who elected Comyn? And was his 'pusillanimity' at Falkirk a recommendation? We know the nature of the next election at Peebles on 19 August 1299, when the assembly was a scene of violence, and the Guardians practically elected themselves by way of temporary accommodation of their warring ambitions.

The election of Comyn, now or subsequently, does not in the smallest degree 'indicate that the charge of treachery is of later concoction'. The positive and strong assertions of the Scots chroniclers are not to be so lightly set aside. One does not expect an English chronicler to mar the glory of the English king by any mention of extraneous aid of such a quality. Yet Hemingburgh remarks a fact that is at any rate very suggestive. He says it was Earl Patrick and the Earl of Angus who brought the news of the Scots position to Bishop Bek, and then the three introduced a youth to tell the king the information he was supposed to have spied out. Earl Patrick and the Earl of Angus were nearly related to Comyn, and the Comyn envy of Wallace was undoubtedly intense and bitter. Yet Comyn did not go over to Edward; on the contrary, he was presently made a Guardian of Scotland. Did Comyn scheme to get rid of Wallace, either by the sword of the English in a hopeless battle or by the unpopularity attendant on a great military disaster? We should be glad to discover some less dastardly reason for his ignominious conduct at Falkirk.

There is great unanimity among the Scots chroniclers that, apart from the treachery of Comyn and his adherents, the essential cause of the disaster at Falkirk was the action of Robert Bruce. They say that the schiltrons resisted every attempt to force them until Bruce and Bek came round in the rear and broke the line. This is a fine illustration of the irony of fate, but it is not history. Bruce was certainly not on the field, neither was he at this time in Edward's allegiance. Scarcely a month before (24 June) Edward had ordered his goods and chattels in Essex to be sold up. It is possible that this very grave blunder arose from confusing Bruce with Basset and a flank with a rear attack. Presently too, Bruce was elected one of the Guardians in the name of Balliol – 'one of those historical phenomena which are inexplicable,' says Hailes rather helplessly.

The remnants of the Scots army drew off from Falkirk towards the north, burning the town and castle of Stirling as they passed. So far Edward pursued them. Having repaired the castle and garrisoned it with Northumbrians, he is said to have harried St Andrews and St Johnston. He then passed through Selkirk Forest to the west, where he found that Bruce had burnt down Ayr Castle, and retired into Carrick, but he could not pursue for lack of provisions. Continuing his journey through Annandale, Edward took and burned Lochmaben Castle. At Carlisle he held a parliament and distributed lands in Scotland to his officers – lands in prospect rather than in possession. Having arranged affairs at Durham and Tynemouth, he settled down at Cottingham to spend Christmas near the comforting shrine of St John of Beverley.

Shortly after Falkirk, whether at the Scots Water or at a convention in St Johnston, Wallace is said to have resigned voluntarily the office of Guardian of Scotland. The Scots writers attribute this step to his recognition of the impossibility of maintaining the independence of his country in cooperation with the jealous nobles. There is much reason to accept this explanation. Not one of the brood could be relied on, except to undermine his authority. He may therefore have determined to stand by himself henceforth as he had done before, aided by such as might choose to attach themselves to his standard. In the political conditions of the time this result would be not only not surprising but, to all appearance, inevitable. The envy and malice of the magnates, the natural leaders of the nation, had driven from the wheel of state the one man who was then capable of steering the shattered barque to a safe and quiet haven.

Comyn and Soulis are said to have been the new Guardians, and in place of Soulis, Lamberton and Bruce were added at Peebles in August 1299. Yet it may be worthwhile to keep an open eye for further light on the question whether Wallace did not remain Guardian till near the latter date, resigning only in view of his purpose to visit France.

CHAPTER VI

WALLACE IN FRANCE

'Cheerly to sea!'
Shakespeare, *King Henry V*, II, 2
'Sanct Androw mot ws speid!'
Harry, ix, 120

There is not a little consensus that Wallace proceeded to France after the battle of Falkirk, but at the same time this part of his career is obscure.

Harry does not hesitate to send Wallace to France, not once only, but twice. The first visit extends from 21 April to the end of August in some year when Wallace was Guardian and shortly before the battle of Blackearnside. Wallace departs without publicly announcing his intention, partly because he was aware that strong objections would be raised to his going, partly because the English would be sure to take measures to intercept him. Leaving the Steward as his substitute, he sailed in a fine new barge from Kirkcudbright with fifty men. The next morning he met with an adventure. The Red Rover hove in sight, but the redoubtable pirate was forced to strike his flag to Wallace, who spared his life. He turned out to be a Frenchman, named Thomas de Longueville, who had hung out his 'red blazon' because of injustices he had suffered. He received a pardon and knighthood, on

Wallace's suggestion, from the French king. Ever afterwards he stood firmly by Wallace and eventually he became lord of Kinfauns near Perth, where he founded, or continued by marriage with the heiress, the family of Charteris.

Landing at Rochelle, Wallace proceeded to Paris where he was cordially received by the French king. He soon tired of inaction, however, and getting together some 900 Scots, went to fight the English at Guienne, his chief exploits being the capture of Schenoun (?Chinon) and Bordeaux. Meantime, the Scots at home, being hard pressed, dispatched Guthrie to urge him to return. Guthrie sailed from Arbroath to Sluys and on reaching Wallace, brought him back by Paris to Sluys and landed him at Montrose. Wallace had been absent for a little over four months.

The second visit Harry places immediately after Wallace's resignation of the Guardianship, shortly after Falkirk. Wallace, he says, sailed from Dundee in a merchant ship with eighteen companions. Again he met with an adventure. Off the mouth of the Humber he encountered a pirate, an Englishman this time, John of Lynn. Putting the crew down in the hold out of his way, he engaged the pirate 18 to 140, boarded him and killed him. From Sluys, Wallace passed through Flanders to Paris, where the king offered him the lordship of Guienne, which he declined. Again he proceeds to Guienne; again he captures Schenoun, and again he besieges Bordeaux. While staying at Schenoun, he finds that there is treachery in France as well as in Scotland. Sent for by the king, he remains in the royal household for two years, and even here he at length finds traitors at work. He will stay no longer. The king gives him letters that had come from Scotland urging his return, loads him with presents and reluctantly parts with him. Wallace sails from Sluys and, passing up the Tay, lands at the mouth of the Earn.

The two visits are so similar in incident that there is something to be said for regarding them as variants of a single visit. The specific date of the first visit must be wrong; nor is it easy to believe that Wallace would have left the kingdom secretly – unless by 'secretly' Harry means what Sir Robert Hastings means by 'without leave' – or have deputed the Steward to fill his place. In itself, there is nothing improbable in the story of the Red Rover, which Sir Walter Scott incorporated in *The Fair Maid of Perth* as 'given by an ancient and uniform tradition, which carries in it great indications of truth, and is warrant enough for its insertion in graver histories than' that historical romance. The second visit is complicated by one of Harry's specific appeals to his 'auctor'; he rests his narrative of Blair's exploits in the sea fight on the account inserted by Gray (who represents himself as an eye-witness) in the book that Harry professes to follow. In any case, Wallace could hardly have spent two years at the French court. In the existing lack of adequate criticism of Harry, one can only reproduce the substance of the stories.

If the author of the *Muses' Threnodie* might be supposed to be independent of Harry's influence, some interest can be attached to the following verses:

> 'I marvell our recòrds nothing at all
> Do mention Wallace going into France.
> How that can be forgote I greatlie scance;
> For well I know all Gasconie and Guien
> Do hold that Wallace was a mightie
> Gian Even to this day; in Rochel likewise found
> A towre from Wallace' name greatly renown'd.'

The French trouvères are said to have exercised their poetic skill on the exploits of Wallace, but little help can be derived from this direction.

It is difficult to feel on more solid ground with the annalist – Rishanger or another – when he states that Wallace, with five knights, went to France after Falkirk to ask aid of Philip; that at Amiens he was ordered by Philip to be imprisoned and kept under observation – an order that the Amiens people cheerfully obeyed, 'for much they loved the King of England'; that Philip offered to deliver him to Edward, and that Edward, with effusive thanks, begged Philip to keep him where he was. There is nothing satisfactory here. Philip might indeed in pressing circumstances have used Wallace as a political pawn, but we know that in fact he treated him very differently. And it is extremely improbable that Edward would have missed such an opportunity of taking his implacable and vexatious foe into his own surer hands. We know how keen he was to catch Lamberton, and Wallace would have been a vastly bigger prize.

More assistance is to be derived from Bishop Stapleton's Kalendar of Treasury documents, compiled about 1323. One interesting entry mentions 'certain letters of safe-conduct granted by Philip King of France, John King of Scotland, and Haco King of Norway, to William Wallace, enabling him to go to the realms of those kings, to sojourn there, and to return; together with certain letters concerning "ordinances and confederations" written to the said William by certain magnates of Scotland.' These letters, it is added, were found on Wallace when he was captured and were delivered to Edward at Kingston by Sir John de Segrave. They are now, unhappily, lost. The dates are not preserved in the Kalendar entry. It is impossible, therefore, to do more than guess at the circumstances of Wallace's proposed visit; and, so far as the entry goes, we can only be certain that he seriously entertained the purpose of visiting France – and possibly Norway – not that he actually carried out such a purpose.

The inference that Wallace positively did visit France may, however, be safely drawn from an existing letter of recommendation in his favour, translated as follows:

> 'Philip, by the grace of God, King of the French, to my beloved and trusty agents appointed to the court of Rome, greeting and love. We command you to request the Supreme Pontiff to hold our beloved William Wallace of Scotland, Knight, recommended to his favour in those matters of business that he has to dispatch with him. Given at Pierrepont on Monday after the Feast of All Saints.'

This document shows that Wallace had intended to proceed to Rome, no doubt to urge the pope to stronger action in favour of Scotland as against the encroachments of Edward. And it seems beyond reasonable doubt that he was already at the court of Philip when he obtained it. The absence of the year date is very tantalizing.

Yet, may it not be fixed with fair certainty? On 20 August 1299, Sir Robert Hastings, the castellan of Roxburgh, reported to Edward an account of the stormy meeting of the Scots nobles at Peebles on the preceding day, when, among other excitements, Sir David de Graham demanded the lands and goods of Sir William Wallace, 'as he was going abroad without leave.' True, Wallace's 'going abroad' may be nothing more than a reported intention, the report not being necessarily trustworthy, although no doubt honestly believed. Yet Sir Malcolm Wallace was present and would probably have known, but although he withstood Sir David, the grounds are not stated. It seems extremely probable, however, that Wallace's reported intention was a fact. If so, Philip's letter of recommendation would readily fall to 1299.

Burton regrets 'that there is nothing to inform us distinctly whether the scraps of evidence alluded to are or are not connected with eminent diplomatic services performed by the popular hero.' There can be no reasonable question that they are connected with a specific effort of Wallace's at least to attempt to perform diplomatic services. It may be taken as certain that Wallace did not go to France on private business or even in disgust with the nobles. Lamberton had just returned from a substantially unsuccessful mission to France, and it seems extremely likely that Wallace had determined to go and see what he could do in person.

It is historically certain then that Wallace visited Philip at least once, that he intended to visit the pope and perhaps the king of Norway, if he did not actually do so, and that he used every possible opportunity on such visits to further the interests of Scotland to the utmost of his power. It is apparently beyond doubt that his mission was not official, but, in any case, his fame would give him a hardly less influential standing. The pope's spurt of brave policy about the time Wallace would have been in Rome may entitle us to consider him among the 'enemies of peace' Edward then complained of so bitterly. Scanty as the facts are, such inferences seem historically reasonable if not inevitable.

CHAPTER VII

𝒯HE LEADERSHIP OF
THE BARONS

'Right to devoted Caledon
The storm of war rolls slowly on,
   With menace deep and dread.'
           Scott, *Lord of the Isles*, VI, 5
'All day with fruitless strife they toil'd. . . .
Rent was the sail, and strain'd the mast,
And many a leak was gaping fast,
And the pale steersman stood aghast,
    And gave the conflict o'er.'
           Ibid. I, 18.

The victor of Falkirk was received in London with extravagant demonstrations of rejoicing. Little did the Fishmongers of the city, who were foremost in ostentation, know that Falkirk was a lucky accident, that the king and all his host had just previously been on the point of retirement, and that after the battle they had had to beat a decently expeditious retreat before the terrors of starvation. The north was solidly in the hands of the Scots. The south, apart from strongholds, was but nominally under the control of the English. The English, in fact, did little more than hold the mere ground they stood on. Nor was the spirit of the Scots broken.

On the contrary, Edward no sooner began to retire than the Scots swarmed after him over the Forth line. Within a fortnight of Falkirk, and only three days after Edward had received homages in Newcastle-under-Ayr, they were in Glasgow, before Edinburgh and in Selkirk Forest. On 9 August, Sir John de Kingston, the Constable of Edinburgh Castle, wrote a most suggestive dispatch to the Lord Treasurer. 'The Earl of Buchan, the Bishop of St Andrews, and other great earls and lords, who were on the other side of the Scots water, have come,' he says, 'to this side. Today they are in Glasgow. They intend to go towards the borders, as is reported among them and their people who are in the Forest. They of the Forest,' adds Sir John, 'have surrendered themselves to the Scots.' Besides, another party had 'suddenly come before our Castle' of Edinburgh and apparently had done some execution, for 'Sir Thomas d'Arderne was taken.' Edward's mighty expedition had, in fact, been no more than a huge foray.

This dispatch of Kingston's is interesting also as casting strong suspicion on a famous soldier of those times, Sir Simon Fraser, whose loyalty to Edward since May 1297 had been conspicuous and valuable. Fraser had accompanied Edward to Flanders and won golden opinions of the king, who had restored his lands in both countries and otherwise made much of him. At this time he was Warden of Selkirk Forest. He had written to Kingston to come to him 'on the day on which our enemies suddenly came before our Castle, and on which Sir Thomas d'Arderne was taken; wherefore,' Kingston warns the Lord Treasurer, 'I fear that he is not of such good faith as he ought to be,' and 'I beg of you and the rest of the King's Council to beware.' More than that:

'Whereas Sir Simon Fraser comes to you in such haste, let me inform you, Sire, that he has no need to be in such a great hurry, for there was not by any means such a great power of people who came into his jurisdiction but that they might have been stopped by the garrisons if Sir Simon had given them warning. And of this I warned him eight days before they came; and before they entered into the Forest, it was reported that there was a treaty between them and Sir Simon, and that they had a conference together, and ate and drank, and were on the best of terms. Wherefore, Sire, it were well that you should be very cautious as to the advice which he should give you.'

Fraser's view of the signs of the times, if not mistakenly represented by Kingston, would further show how slight was the English hold on Scotland.

During the remainder of the year, large quantities of provisions and war material were pressed forward to the castles south of the Forth; each castle made a foray as it found opportunity, and occasionally combined forays were made with special precautions, particularly into Selkirk Forest. One of the most important of these combined expeditions, devised at Berwick on 1 December, was to start about the middle of the month for Stirling, which was in need of supplies. Sir John de Kingston was head organizer, and horses were requisitioned as far south as Norham. In these arrangements, full confidence appears to be extended by the king to Sir Simon Fraser. It may also be noted that on 19 November Earl Patrick had been appointed Captain of the Forces and Castles on the East March of Scotland south of the Forth.

The summonses for the next year's expedition against Scotland were issued in good time. On 26 September the army was ordered to assemble at Carlisle on Whitsun eve. On 12 December orders were issued to various sheriffs and other officers in England to forward provisions to Berwick, and to the high officers of state in Ireland to forward provisions to Skinburness, in each case by the same date (6 June). Edward was in hot mood. He was determined to attack the malignant rebels next summer 'in great power' and to annihilate them (*in eorum summum exterminium*). The language of his writs is somewhat difficult to reconcile with praise of his tenderness and sense of justice. The great expedition, however, did not start at Whitsunday, as Edward had proposed in the preceding September. Barons had proved recalcitrant, and the king's wrangles with them over further ratification of the great Charter had been kept up through the year until Edward was compelled to yield to their demands.

One of the annalistic records ascribed to Rishanger states that Wallace, together with his brother – probably Sir Malcolm – the Earl of Athol and many others, lay in hiding after Falkirk. That is to say, finding open opposition impossible, Wallace resumed his guerrilla tactics. No doubt he had separated himself from the untrustworthy nobles and determined to maintain resistance as and how his men and means would allow him.

In the early summer of 1299, Lamberton had gone to the court of France, probably at the instance of Wallace, to seek the aid of Philip. Edward got news of this, and between 10 June and 20 August, he issued safe-conducts in favour of the masters of half a dozen vessels of Winchelsea and Rye whom he had directed to keep a lookout and intercept the bishop and his company, 'who have already come into Flanders, prepared to go into Scotland.' The attempt was unsuccessful.

Lamberton's mission, however, did not prove fruitful, at least directly. Through the good offices of the pope, peace had been patched up between Edward and Philip, and indeed there were already in negotiation two royal marriages – one between Edward and Philip's half-sister Margaret, which was celebrated at Canterbury in the following October, and one between Prince Edward and Philip's infant daughter Isabella, who were betrothed on 20 May 1303 and married on 25 January 1308.

During Lamberton's absence, Wallace was no doubt actively engaged, although there remain no records to show clearly how or where. It may be that this is the occasion when John the Marshal, bailiff of the Earl of Lincoln in the barony of Renfrew, dispatched to Edward an urgent request for aid. The Guardian of Scotland, with 300 men-at-arms and a multitude of foot, who had lurked in Galloway, he says, had entered Cunningham after the king's son, had taken his bailiffs with other freeholders there and had made a fine for their heads and had totally rebelled against their late fealty. Unless he have immediate aid, he cannot defend the barony against so many Scots. To the same time evidently belong undated petitions to the king from the Abbot and convent of Sweetheart, and from the Abbey of Our Lady of Dundrennan, which show that the English power in Galloway was totally inadequate to stem the advances of the Scots. Was Wallace still 'the Guardian of Scotland'? Or does the incident belong to 1300 or 1301, the (local) 'Guardian' being Comyn?

It was probably Lamberton's report that determined Wallace to go to the Continent in person. In spite of occasional successes, it must have appeared to him all but hopeless to maintain any effective resistance to Edward in the divided state of the Scots counsels unless some external aid could be procured, either directly in support of the Scots or indirectly in restraint of Edward. On the failure of his envoy, he seems to have resolved to sheath his sword for a time and to proceed to Paris and, if need were, to Rome in quest of support. There can indeed be no doubt that the inherent weakness of the situation had been pressing severely upon him ever since the battle of Falkirk, and it is likely enough that he had already provided himself with letters of safe-conduct. Was it at this time that he formally resigned the office of Guardian?

On 19 August 1299, there was a remarkable gathering of the Scots nobles at Peebles. An account of the proceedings is given in a letter of 20 August addressed to Edward by Sir Robert Hastings, the castellan of Roxburgh, from information obtained through a spy. The Scots had made a vigorous inroad on Selkirk Forest. The nobles present were 'the Bishop of St Andrews, the Earls of Carrick, Buchan . . . and Menteith, Sir John Comyn the younger, and the Steward of Scotland.' The council board was ringed with dissension. Sir David de Graham demanded Sir William Wallace's lands and goods, because 'he was going abroad without leave.' Sir Malcolm Wallace, however, the hero's brother, interposed objections and presently 'the two knights gave each other the lie and drew their knives.' This was but a prelude. Sir John Comyn took the Earl of Carrick, the future king, by the throat, and the Earl of Buchan laid violent hands on the sacred person of the Bishop of St Andrews.

The question that generated so much heat was an election to the Guardianship. The physical encounters indicate clearly the division of parties: it was a struggle between the Comyn and the Bruce influence. Wallace himself, of course, had washed his hands clean of ambitious nobles, but his bishop naturally stood by Bruce against Comyn. The Bruce party gained the day. The final agreement, as the letter correctly states, was that the Bishop of St Andrews, the Earl of Carrick and Sir John Comyn should be Guardians of the realm, the bishop having custody of the castles as principal. Sir Ingram de Umfraville, who had taken a conspicuous part in the inroad, was made Sheriff of Roxburgh and Sir Robert de Keith Warden of Selkirk Forest, with 100 barbed horse and 1500 foot besides the foresters to make raids on the English march (borderland). Leaving a portion of their men with Umfraville, the lords departed the same day, the Earl of Carrick and Sir David de Brechin going to Annandale and Galloway, the Earl of Buchan and Comyn to the north of Forth, and the Steward and the Earl of Menteith to Clydesdale. The Bishop of St Andrews was to stay in the meantime at Stobo. The election was obviously a mere arrangement between the parties, backed by their immediate henchmen, but that did not hinder them from speaking, in their official documents, in the name of the community of the realm.

Edward was as eager as ever to quell the perverse Scots. On 18 September he summoned a levy of 16,000 men to assemble at Newcastle-upon-Tyne by 24 November. He was still delayed, however, by his recalcitrant barons, and on 16 November he issued a fresh summons for his army to meet him at Berwick on 13 December. Meantime the Scots Guardians, who were besieging Stirling, had intimated to him on 13 November their willingness to cease hostilities on the basis of the proposals the king of France had made to him. Edward ignored their offer, however, and proceeded to Berwick with the determination of raising the siege of Stirling. But at Berwick his magnates proved intractable and he was compelled to abandon Stirling to its fate and return to London. The garrison of Stirling soon afterwards surrendered, having suffered cruel privations.

Nor was Edward more successful at the other end of the border. During the summer immense supplies had been landed at Skinburness and stored at Carlisle from which Lochmaben was largely furnished. Raids had been made into Galloway in force, yet the Scots had cut off convoys at the Solway. From Carlaverock Castle they had even seriously menaced Lochmaben. Sir Robert de Felton tells how Carlaverock 'has done and does great damage every day to the King's castle and people', adding the gratifying intelligence that on the Sunday next after Michaelmas he had had the pleasure of adorning the great tower of Lochmaben with the head of the Carlaverock Constable, Sir Robert de Cunningham, a near relative of the Steward's. In December, Warenne, with some of the greatest English barons, conducted to the western march an expedition consisting (or intended to consist) of some 500 barbed horse (with 200 more if they could be got) and over 8000 foot. But this enterprise also proved abortive. The Scots were yet to be subdued, and Edward, on 29 December, issued summonses for the next year's campaign, the army to muster at Carlisle on 1 July. Rishanger's summary of the year is suggestive: '*Scotis perfidia notabili*', the year of 'outstanding Scots treachery'.

In 1300 the vexatious English raids were repeated with similar results. In mid-July Edward advanced from Carlisle and besieged Lochmaben, which had fallen into the hands

141

of the Scots. Having taken Lochmaben, he moved on Carlaverock, which refused his demand of unconditional surrender; whereupon he raged 'like a lioness robbed of her whelps,' besieged the castle and took it. He then marched into Galloway, Prince Edward and Warenne with him. Lochmaben and Carlaverock notwithstanding, he was in a very gloomy mood. The Bishop of Witherne and two knights came to treat for peace: he would do nothing. Again they approached him at the bridge of Dee: still he would do nothing. Then, at Kirkcudbright, the Earl of Buchan and Sir John Comyn treated with him for a day, and again for another day: all in vain. Their terms, it is said, were these: that Balliol should be restored and the succession vested in his son Edward (Sir John Comyn's wife was Balliol's daughter Marjory) and that the Scots nobles should have the right to redeem such of their lands as Edward had bestowed on Englishmen. Otherwise they would defend themselves as long as they might. Edward was exceedingly angry and repelled their demands.

The Scots accordingly harassed his retreat. Some severe fighting took place. A Scots deserter is said to have led some 200 of the English into a trap on pretence of enabling them to surprise the enemy, and although the Scots were at last defeated and fled 'like hares before harriers', Edward was not comforted. Day by day he was eating out his heart because of his lack of success. His Welsh troops deserted. Many of his nobles even, seeing the futility of the enterprise, and writhing under lack of money and necessaries, requested leave to go home, and, on the king's refusal, they too deserted. In this emergency, baffled to know what to do against the accursed Scots (*contra nefandam gentem Scotorum*), he appealed to his friends for counsel. One noted the approach of winter; another recalled the punishment inflicted on the enemy; a third impressed the expediency of releasing at any rate some of his followers. The enterprise of the year was clearly over. But Edward, with stubborn tenacity, not to say wilfulness, would remain yet awhile in Galloway. Then he would winter in Carlisle and return to crush the perverse nation in the spring. And some of his earls stood by him in the dreary and futile delay. At last, on the interposition of Philip, a truce was ratified at Dumfries on 30 October, to run from Hallowmas to Whitsunday. The expedition had proved an inglorious failure. Rishanger's summary of the year is this: '*Sollicitus propter rebellionem Scotiae*', 'troubled on account of the rebellion of the Scots'.

On 27 June 1299, the pope had issued a bull to Edward, claiming Scotland as from ancient times and now a fief of the Holy See, and not now or ever a fief of the English king, ordering the instant release of the Bishop of Glasgow and other Scots ecclesiastics from English prisons and demanding the surrender of the castles, and especially of the religious houses, in Scotland. The bull was an abnormal time on the road: it seems to have taken the best part of a year to reach the Archbishop of Canterbury, who was instructed to deliver it into the king's own hand, and the archbishop, whose adventures Burton details with grave humour, did not succeed in executing his commission until towards the end of August 1300.

The barons took up the matter with clear decision; 104 of them, in parliament at Lincoln on 12 February 1301, firmly rejected the pope's claim in the most absolute terms. Edward, in outward respect for his Holiness, again had the monasteries ransacked for information, sent to Oxford and Cambridge for doctors of the civil law and set forth an elaborate statement of his case, concluding with the assertion of his absolute and indefeasible title to the realm of Scotland in property as well as in possession. The document is dated 7 May 1301. It is an extraordinary example of solemn diplomatic fooling in reckless defiance and omission of essential facts. The answer of the Scots envoy, Baldred Bisset, partly followed the same lines but dealt fatal blows to every substantial element of argument. Edward's only firm ground was conquest, and the conquest of Scotland was the one point in practical dispute.

In May the Scots and French envoys were to be in conference with Edward's commissioners at Canterbury with a view to peace with Scotland. But early in April, Edward, to make sure of the event, warned his magnates in the north, 'on the expiry of the truce to be ready on the march to resist the attacks of the Scots, if necessary.' The expression is curiously defensive. However, on 12 May he had become satisfied of the necessity and issued orders for a levy of some 12,000 men. His actual force on the expedition consisted of little more than half that number – about 6800, all on foot, except their officers and a few light horsemen or hobelars. On 6–18 July Edward was at Berwick; 2–14 August at Peebles; 21 August to 4 September at Glasgow; 27 September to 27 October mostly at Dunipace, also at Stirling; 1 November to 31 January at Linlithgow, where he built a peel, and on 19 February he repassed the border into England. The main fact recorded by the chroniclers is the loss of horses through lack of forage and the severity of the northern winter.

The campaign, in fact, was conducted at cross-purposes. The Scots avoided the English army and practised guerrilla tactics. In September Sir Robert de Tilliol, the castellan of Lochmaben, was in great straits and thankful for a promise of relief. 'And we give you to understand as a certainty,' he writes to the king, 'that John de Soulis and the Earl of Buchan, with their power, are lying at Loudon; and Sir Simon Fraser at Stonehouse, and Sir Alexander de Aber-nethy and Sir Herbert de Morham.' If the king would only send a hundred armed horse, with a good leader, tomorrow at the latest! 'But' – and at this time Edward was probably in Glasgow – 'be informed that all the country is rising because we have no troops to ride upon them.' On 7 September Sir John de Soulis and Sir Ingram de Umfraville, with over 7000 men, actually burnt Lochmaben and assaulted the peel, and next day they made another attempt. Sustaining some severe losses, however, they turned away towards Nithsdale and Galloway. 'They cause to return to them,' says Sir Robert, 'those persons who had come to the peace, and they are collecting greater force to come to our marches.' A few days later Sir Robert Hastings was on the lookout for this body of Scots about Roxburgh.

Again, on 3 October, the Constable of Newcastle-on-Ayr wrote to the king that 'the Scots were in Carrick, before the Castle of Turnberry, with 400 men-at-arms, and within these eight days had wanted to attack Ayr Castle.' He accordingly begs for speedy succour, 'for the Scots are in such force that he and the other loyalists there cannot withstand them.' In February Newcastle-on-Ayr was besieged by the Scots, and the garrison 'could noways go out with safety, and lost some in their long stay.'

But in all these excursions and alarms there was nothing decisive. One cannot imagine that, with anything like 7000 men at his back, Wallace would have allowed Edward, with only a slightly larger and not so very much better armed force, to winter comfortably at Linlithgow. Edward, in any case, went bootless home. On 26 January at Linlithgow, on the interposition of the French king, he had ratified a truce with the Scots to last until St Andrew's Day (30 November) 1302. The year, according to Rishanger, had been 'Scotis suspiciosus turbidus inquietus' 'suspicious, disorderly restless Scots'.

Edward himself clearly felt that nothing solid had been accomplished and bent again to the task. He had only reached Morpeth on his return journey, when, on 23 February, he expressed to a large number of his lords his wish to prepare – in case the truce worked no amendment in the Scots – for an expedition that should be vigorous and final. The high Irish officials, in particular, were directed to bestir themselves.

In 1302, Lamberton again paid an official visit to Philip and brought back a letter with him dated 6 April. Philip's letter is addressed to the Guardians, the magnates, 'and the whole community, his dear friends,' to whom he 'wishes health and hope of fortitude in adversity.' It was summarized it thus:

> 'He received with sincere affection their envoys, John, Abbot of Jeddwurth [Jedburgh], and John Wissard, Knight, and fully understands their letters and messages anxiously expressed by the envoys. Is moved to his very marrow by the evils brought on their country through hostile malignity. Praises them for their constancy to their King and their shining valour in de-

fence of their native land against injustice, and urges them to persevere in the same course. Regarding the aid which they ask, he is not unmindrul of the old league between their King, themselves, and him, and is carefully pondering ways and means of helping them. But, bearing in mind the dangers of the road, and dreading the risks which sometimes chance to letters, he has given his views by word of mouth to W[illiam], Bishop of St Andrews, for whom he asks full credence.'

Philip would if he could, at any rate in words; but his truce with Edward had been steadily renewed and restrained his ardour in the cause of Scotland. He had already burnt the pope's offensive bull, however, and the great quarrel between these potentates was hot. Pope Boniface accordingly had drawn towards Edward. On 13 August he had addressed bulls to the Bishop of Glasgow (for whom he had doughtily taken Edward to task in 1299) and to the other Scots bishops, menacingly exhorting them to peaceful ways and administering a special wigging to the shifty Wishart, whom he likened to 'a rock of offence and a stone of stumbling.' But Edward, his 'dearly beloved son in Christ', astutely temporized with his urgent representations in favour of a resumption of war with France. Still the pope's anxious desire for Edward's favour relaxed the modicum of restraint he had exercised upon Edward's aggression on the Scots.

In April, Bruce appears to have gone over to Edward again. On the 28th Edward writes of 'his liege Robert de Brus, Earl of Carrick', and of special favour he restores to Bruce's tenants their lands in England lately taken for their rebellion, and grants to Patrick de Trumpe the younger and his aunt, Matilda de Carrick, two of such tenants, certain

147

lands in the manor of Levington in Cumberland to which they had fallen heirs.

The campaign of 1302 was entrusted by Edward to Sir John de Segrave. On 29 September Segrave was ordered to execute with all haste a foray, lately arranged with Sir Ralph de Manton, by Stirling and Kirkintilloch. On 20 January Edward sent to his aid Sir Ralph Fitz William, having heard from Segrave and others 'that for certain the Scots rebels, in increased force, have broken into the lands there in his possession, occupied certain castles and towns, and perpetrated other excesses; and, unless checked, they may break into England as usual.'

He was destined soon to hear worse news. Segrave's army, marching in three divisions, was suddenly attacked by Comyn and Fraser, who made a forced night march from Biggar and came upon the first division at daybreak of 24 February in the neighbourhood of Roslin. The division was totally defeated, and Segrave himself was seriously wounded and captured. The second division coming up shared the fate of the first. The third division, who had meanwhile been at their devotions, succeeded (according to the English accounts) in repulsing the Scots 'in great measure' and in recovering some of the prisoners. The Scots chroniclers make a big affair of it and report the English as worsted in all three encounters. In any case, it was the main body of the English army that was surprised and routed, and it must have been a fight of considerable magnitude. Sir Ralph de Manton, the Cofferer or Paymaster, was among the slain.

Rishanger attributes the rising of the Scots to the action of Wallace, who had been appointed their leader and captain, but there is probably some confusion in this and stronger authority is needed to induce belief in any association of Wallace with the movements of Comyn. Rishanger sums up the year as '*Scotis odibilis, detestabilis, et invisus*', 'abominable, hated and detested Scots'.

In the meantime, seven envoys from Scotland were in Paris with the object of gaining effective aid from Philip. They were William Lamberton, Bishop of St Andrews; Matthew Crambeth, Bishop of Dunkeld; the Earl of Buchan; the Steward; Sir John de Soulis; Sir Ingram de Umfraville and Sir William de Balliol. They appear, as Hailes judges, 'to have been the dupes of the policy of the French court'. On 25 May they report to Sir John Comyn the conclusion of a final peace between France and England (20 May), the Scots being excluded. That very significant omission, they urge, should not alarm their friends in Scotland. For Philip will at once dispatch envoys to Edward to draw him back from war on the Scots and to procure a truce, pending a personal conference of the kings, when a peace favourable to the Scots will be concluded, if not previously effected by the envoys. Philip had positively assured them on this point.

The real reason for the exclusion of the Scots is simply this, that their case will be more easily settled between the two kings when these are united in friendship and affinity, Prince Edward and the Princess Isabella being now betrothed. They are urged by Philip to remain so as to carry back a good result of their errand – not, of course, to keep them out of the field against Edward. The fame of the late conflict has spread over the whole world; let them, therefore, in case of Edward's refusal of a truce, for the Lord's sake, not despair but act with resolution. As Hailes remarks, the letter 'exhibits a characteristical portrait of fortitude and credulity.' Edward ratified his treaty with France on 10 June (?July) at St Johnston!

On 9 April Edward ordered a levy of 9500 men in England, and about the same time summoned Bruce to bring 1000 foot from Carrick and Galloway and Sir Richard Siward to bring 300 from Nithsdale. On 16 May the king was at Roxburgh where he remained to the end of the month. He marched north by Edinburgh and Linlithgow and stayed at Perth (St Johnston), with occasional excursions, from 10 June to the end of July. By Brechin and Aberdeen, he passed on to Banff, Cullen and Elgin and rested at Kinloss in Moray from 13 September to 4 October. On 6 November he was back at Dunfermline where he remained until 4 March 1304.

Edward's progress through Scotland met with no opposition except at Brechin, where Sir Thomas de Maule maintained a heroic resistance until he was killed on the castle wall. Hemingburgh says the advance of the army was marked by burning and devastation. Burton, however, thinks such violence was inconsistent with Edward's policy, which then led him to avoid exasperating the people. 'Had there been much wanton cruelty or destruction,' he says, 'it would have left its mark somewhere in contemporary documents.' The inference is hardly a safe one, in any case. There does exist, however, another significant record – an order of Edward's, dated Dunfermline, 18 November 1303, directing his Chancellor to issue a pardon in favour of Warin Martyn. Martyn, it is recited, had very often been leader of the Welshmen in the king's army in Scotland and had represented that these men, in coming and going, had perpetrated murders, robberies, arsons and other felonies, under his leadership, and that he could not altogether do justice on them. He had therefore supplicated a pardon, fearing that these deeds might subsequently be brought up against him. It is not readily credible that Edward could keep a tight hand on his soldiery any more than Comyn or Wallace – or Warin Martyn. Then there is the burning of Dunfermline Abbey.

For several weeks negotiations for a peace were carried on between Edward and Comyn, and at length a peace was settled at Strathord on 9 February. The terms were remarkably easy for the Scots, possibly because Edward was in a gracious mood, much more probably because he felt that the coming siege of Stirling Castle would absorb his undivided attention. The one prominent Scot who did not submit was Sir William Wallace. The terms of peace will be more conveniently noted in the next chapter, in connection with the striking basis laid down by Edward for their eventual mitigation.

It was in March 1304, on Edward's departure, that 'Dunfermline saw its Abbey red with flames'. The burning of this magnificent house has been variously characterized as 'atrocious', 'barbarous', 'unscrupulous and vindictive', and so forth. A Westminster chronicler appears to hold undisputed the bad eminence of attempting to justify the deed. The Abbey, he explains, was spacious enough to lodge at one and the same time conveniently three mighty kings and their retinues. But there was an accursed taint on the place. Its size had rendered it suitable for the Scots nobles to hold their meetings there; and there they had devised machinations against the English king; and thence, in time of war, they issued as from ambush to harry and murder the English. What then? The king's army, therefore, perceiving that the temple of the Lord was not a church, but a den of robbers, a

151

thorn as it were in the eye of the English nation, fired the buildings. The church and a few cells for monks – this was all that remained of the venerable and magnificent Abbey capable of receiving three mighty kings together.

But there was another thorn in the eye of Edward and that was the Castle of Stirling. On 1 April he commanded the Earls of Strathearn, Menteith and Lennox to see to it that none of their people should go to the castle to buy or sell provisions or merchandise, to carry any victuals to the garrison or indeed to hold any communication with them. On 6 April 'engines' – siege equipment, like battering rams – were shipped from Edinburgh. On the same day more engines and materials were dispatched from Berwick. On 16 April Sir John Botetourte is directed to aid Bruce in forwarding 'the frame of the great engine of Inverkip', which Bruce had just reported as unmanageable, and on 21 April Sir Robert de Leyburne, Constable of Inverkip Castle, is ordered 'to arrest at Glasgow all the iron and great stones of the engines there, and forward them to Stirling, without any manner of excuse or delay,' for by the inaction in these parts 'the siege is greatly delayed.' On 12 April the king had ordered the Prince of Wales 'to procure and take as much lead as you can about the town of St John of Perth and Dunblane, and elsewhere, as from the churches and from other places where you can find it, provided always that the churches be not uncovered over the altars.' In the first half of April, Edward had spent several days before the walls, and on 22 April he definitely opened the siege.

In the immensity of war material that had been laboriously brought up, there were at least thirteen powerful engines, war machines capable of throwing weights of 100,

200 and 300 pounds, besides the 'War-wolf', a novel machine that apparently was not quite ready for action. The garrison appear to have improvised some machines of offence, for both Rishanger and Hemingburgh record that they killed many of the besiegers with their engines. Edward entered into the conduct of operations with the old fire of younger times. One day, as he was riding about and directing his men, he was shot with an arrow that stuck in his armour but did not wound him.

Towards the end of June, the English appear to have been hard pressed for forage. The king's horses, according to one correspondent, 'have nothing to eat but grass'; there is 'the utmost need of oats and beans'. And in another letter of the same date, the same writer urges the addressee – probably Sir Richard de Bremesgrave – 'to send all the king's stores he can find in Berwick, in haste by day and night, to Stirling, for they can find nothing in these parts.' At the same time Edward was still summoning from England crossbowmen and carpenters.

The garrison made a spirited and resolute defence. Every day Edward had the dykes filled with branches of trees and logs of wood, and every day the garrison fired them. Then he filled up the dykes with stones and earth and pushed the scaling machines up to the walls. Thereupon the garrison, who were in desperate straits from hunger, offered to capitulate on terms of life and limb. Edward, however, insisted on absolute submission. At last, on 20 July 1304, the garrison surrendered. They are said to have numbered 140, but, besides the gallant Constable, Sir William Oliphant, there are only twenty-five others, including two friars, mentioned in the instrument attesting the surrender. Before evacuation, a strange ceremony took place, partly for scientific experiment, partly to amuse the English ladies. The king ordered that none of his people should enter the castle until it should be struck with the 'War-wolf'; those within might defend themselves from the 'Wolf' as best they could! Oliphant, who had been captured in Dunbar Castle and kept in prison in Devizes Castle until 8 September 1297, was now sent back to England and lodged in the Tower of London. The rest of the garrison were distributed to various English castles. Edward returned to England towards the end of August.

The four years' warfare of the barons – we may say, of Comyn – had not advanced the cause of independence. Still it had deferred submission. Bruce, apparently influenced by some matter of property in England, possibly galled by friction with Comyn, had again bowed to Edward early in 1302. Lamberton had confined himself to diplomacy and administration; Comyn had practically the whole direction of military affairs. Both had exerted themselves creditably, but both of them submitted to Edward in 1304. They displayed neither brilliance nor endurance. They lacked the qualities of leaders in the forlorn state of the kingdom.

From the autumn of 1299 to 1303–4, no definite share in the desultory warfare can be assigned confidently to Wallace. If the movement that culminated in the victory of Roslin in 1302 may be ascribed to him, on the authority of Rishanger, yet it would be rash to believe that he was on the field of battle. It may rather be taken as certain that he did not act in concert with Comyn. Nor is it easy to suppose that Wallace was in Scotland in 1301 and 1301–2, when Edward was allowed to stay comfortably some three months in Linlithgow with a very small force – a force little stronger than Comyn's

154

officers had about the same time in the southwest. It may be that such points indicate the exhaustion of the country as much as the incapacity of the generals: Langtoft says Comyn and his men (1303–4) 'have nothing to drink, or eat, nor power remaining wherewith to manage war.' One can only fall back on the conviction that Wallace could have used the available materials to far greater advantage, and that, in the circumstances, he had at any rate been doing his best for his country. The surrender of Comyn in 1304 again brought him to the front as the one Scots leader who stood immovably against the invader, resolute to live or to die free men.

CHAPTER VIII

THE BETRAYAL AND DEATH OF WALLACE

'In this caus that I wend,
Sa that we wyn, I rek nocht for till end.
Rycht suth it is that anys we mon de:
In to the rycht, quha suld in terrour be?'
                                    Harry, viii, 171–4

'For chans off wer thou suld no murnyng mak;
As werd will wyrk, thi fortoun mon thou tak.'
                                    Harry, ix, 243–4

'Thi last reward in erd sall be bot small.
Let nocht tharfor, tak rèdress off this myss:
To thi reward thou sall haiff lestand blyss.'
                                    Harry, vii, 102–4

'In the history of the next five years' after the battle of Falkirk, writes Lingard, Wallace's 'name is scarcely ever mentioned.' The suggestion seems to be that Wallace ceased to be an influential factor in the course of events. But after all, Lingard is driven to acknowledge the force of Wallace's personality at the expense of his own consistency. He comes to admit that 'the only man whose enmity could give' Edward a 'moment's uneasiness, was Wallace.' The statement looks remarkably like a reproduction of an English scribe's assertion that after the submission of Comyn and the other nobles there was left but 'one disorderly fellow [*unus ribaldus*], William Wallace by name, who gave the King just a touch of uneasiness' (*aliquntulum fatigavit*). Edward himself, it is plain, had formed a very different estimate of that touch. He was well aware that the other Scots leaders would stand with him or against him according to the strength of his grip on the country; more than once he had seen both sides of the political coats of most of them. The more dangerous of them – three or four – he could muzzle effectively enough by a short period of banishment, during which he would reduce the inflammability of the materials they could work upon. Wallace, however, was a conspicuously more able man than any of the time-servers. He was the one prominent Scot who had never submitted, and he was known to be resolutely irreconcilable. There remained only one course: Wallace must be destroyed.

Edward, with the siege of Stirling before him, would not have been likely to allow resentment to overbear policy in the case of any of the Scots leaders unless he had become convinced that the particular offender was either not worth consideration or else hopelessly recalcitrant. There must, indeed, as Lingard says, have been 'something peculiar' in Wallace's case 'which rendered him less deserving of mercy' than the others. Wallace alone was expressly excluded from the treaty of Strathord. Sir John Comyn, the head and front of the immediate offending, escaped easily by the ignominious door of abject humiliation. The Steward and Sir John de Soulis, who had on previous occasions bent to similar necessities, were let off with two years' banishment south of the

Trent. Sir Simon Fraser and Thomas du Bois – both men who compelled the respect of their opponents – were more severely dealt with, by exile for three years from Scotland, England and France. Yet Edward must have had very distinctly in his mind the mortifying defeat of Roslin, achieved by Comyn and Fraser. The chameleon Bishop of Glasgow, 'for the great harm he has done', was merely banished for two or three years. In any case, these judgments were but slackly enforced, even in those instances where enforcement was within Edward's power. But Wallace – 'he may come in to the King's grace, if he thinks good.' It is idle to speculate what Edward would have done with him if he had then 'come into the King's grace.'

Edward had certainly made attempts to conciliate Wallace. By the agency of Warenne, he did so just before the battle of Stirling. He may even have offered the patriot his royal pardon, with lordships and lands. Bower says he did. He may, although not at all probably, have dangled before him the crown of Scotland under English control. The record of the judgment pronounced on Wallace mentions that after Falkirk the king had 'mercifully caused him to be recalled to his peace'; and the reference is probably to some specific overture and not merely to the general summons. Bower reproduces the story that Wallace's friends now urged his acceptance of the proposed terms and that Wallace thereupon delivered his sentiments as follows:

'O desolate Scotland, over-credulous of deceptive speeches, and little foreseeing the calamities that are coming upon you! If you were to judge as I do, you would not readily place your neck under a foreign yoke. When I was a youth, I learned from my uncle, a priest, this proverb – a proverb worth more than all the riches of the world – and ever since I have marked it in my mind:

> *Dico tibi verum, Libertas optima rerum;*
> *Nunquam servili sub nexu vivito, fili.* ★

And therefore, in a word, I declare that, if all Scotsmen together yield obedience to the King of England, or part each one with his own liberty, yet I and my comrades who may be willing to adhere to me in this behalf, will stand for the freedom of the realm; and, with God's help, we will obey no man but the King, or his lieutenant.'

Whether this striking scene was ever enacted or not, there can be no doubt that the writer represents faithfully the attitude of Wallace. The rejection of the king's proffered clemency, even if but indirectly or generally proffered, would naturally sting his proudly sensitive feeling. In any case, Edward was fully satisfied that he would never have peace in Scotland while Wallace was in the field and that Wallace would regard with contempt his threats and his promises and succumb only to superior force or to insidious policy.

Early in 1304, Edward had made up his mind that he would receive Wallace on no terms short of unconditional surrender, and he was determined to have him in his power at the earliest possible moment. To somewhere very near this period – say February – must probably be assigned an undated draft of letters patent, whereby Edward grants to his 'chier vadlet' (dear vallet), Edward de Keith, afterwards

★ 'The best liberty is never servile;
  Never under bond lives.'

159

Sheriff of Selkirk, all goods and chattels of whatever kind he may gain from Sir William Wallace, the king's enemy, to his own profit and pleasure. At this date, certainly, Edward was putting all irons in the fire to accomplish his intense wish to lay hands upon the redoubtable Wallace.

About this time Wallace and his followers appear to have been hovering not very far away, south of the Forth. Sir Alexander de Abernethy, Warden between the Mounth and the Forth, had been dispatched by the Prince of Wales to Strathearn, Menteith and Drip to guard the passage of the river. Sir Alexander appears to have written to the king on the subject of terms to Wallace. In his answer, dated 3 March, Edward laid down definitively once more the requirement of unconditional submission:

> 'In reply to your request for instructions as to whether it is our pleasure that you should hold out to William Wallace any words of peace, know that it is not at all our pleasure that you hold out any word of peace to him, or to any other of his company, unless they place themselves absolutely (*de haut et de bas*) and in all things at our will without any reservation whatsoever.'

The final corrections of the original draft of this letter indicate how careful Edward was to express his stern resolution with unmistakable precision and emphasis. Wallace must surrender at discretion.

There is nothing to show whether Sir Alexander Abernethy had put the point to Edward of his own motion, in view of contingencies or on the prompting of some application addressed to him from the Scots side. It seems more likely that he was hopeful of success and wished to fortify himself with definite instructions. The first paragraph of the letter shows markedly the king's sense of the importance of Sir Alexander's service: he urges the knight to all possible diligence; he signifies where aid, if necessary, may be had, and he orders that Sir Alexander shall not leave his service in these parts unaccomplished, 'neither for the parliament nor for any other business.' The same day (3 March) Edward wrote to 'his loyal and faithful Robert de Brus,' applauding his diligence on that side the Forth, and urging him, 'as the robe is well made, you will be pleased to make the hood.' Two days later he directed the Prince of Wales to reinforce Abernethy at the fords and passes above Drip, and on 11 March he sent special instructions also to the Earl of Strathearn to see to the guarding of the fords and of the country about, so that none of the enemy might cross to injure the king's lieges on the north side.

The proximity of Wallace, and the hope of putting him down finally, no doubt had a foremost place in Edward's calculations. It does not seem likely, although it may have been the case, that application had been made to Abernethy on behalf of Wallace; perhaps the king's reply would have specifically indicated the fact. It is not to be believed for an instant that any such application would have been made with the sanction or knowledge of Wallace himself.

But for the absurd bias of Langtoft, one might be inclined to connect an episode of his with the negotiations that issued in the treaty of Strathord and with Sir Alexander de Abernethy's letter. After Christmas 1303, Langtoft says, Wallace lay in the forest – the glen of Pittencrieff has been suggested as the particular spot – and 'through friends' made request to the king at Dunfermline 'that he may submit to his honest peace without surrendering into his hands body or head, but that the King grant him, of his gift, not as a loan, an honourable allowance of woods and cattle, and by his writing the seisin and investment for him and his heirs in purchased land.' The whole bent of Wallace's mind was undoubtedly against any such application. Anyhow, 'the King,' says Langtoft, 'angered at this demand, breaks into a rage, commends Wallace to the devil, and all that grows on him, and promises 300 marks to the man that shall make him headless.' Whereupon Wallace takes to the moors and the hills and 'robs for a living.'

Wallace, however, had very different business on hand. Apparently he had found it hopeless to effect the passage of the Forth or to communicate with Stirling Castle. Sir John de Segrave, the Warden south of Forth, had joined hands with Bruce and Clifford to attack him. He had therefore retired into Lothian, Sir Simon Fraser with him and the English force in pursuit. A renegade Scot, John de Musselburgh, guided the English commander to where his countrymen were hiding. Wallace and Fraser were brought to bay at Peebles (Hopperewe) in Tweeddale and defeated. The news was brought to Edward at Aberdour on 12 March, and on 15 March John of Musselburgh received from the gratified king's own hand the noble reward of 10 shillings.

Already Edward was deep in preparations for the siege of Stirling, which, as we have seen, absorbed his whole energies from the middle of March until late in July. On 25 July 1304, the day after the formal surrender of the obstinate castle, he was in high good humour. There has been preserved the roll of the magnates and others who served under him in this campaign, and one of the paragraphs informs us how the king on that day commanded fourteen barons therein named to settle in what manner they and the others on the roll should be rewarded for the services they had rendered. At the same time his mind returned with renewed energy to Sir William Wallace. A later paragraph represents him as attempting to enlist the Scots leaders whose terms of submission had been arranged in the beginning of February, in a comprehensive hunt after Wallace. There is no crude mention of a specific blood price in marks, but on the success of the hunt their own future treatment is made very expressly dependent. Comyn, Lindsay, Graham and Fraser, who had been adjudged to go into exile as well as other Scots liegemen of Edward, were urged to do their endeavour 'between now and the twentieth day after Christmas' to capture Wallace and to deliver him to the king. The king will see how they bear themselves in the business, and will show more favour to the man who shall have captured Wallace by shortening his term of exile, by diminishing the amount of his ransom or of his obligation for trespasses or by otherwise lightening his liabilities. It is further ordained that the Steward, Sir John de Soulis, and Sir Ingram de Umfraville shall not have any letters of safe-conduct to come into the power of the king until Sir William Wallace shall have been surrendered to him. It stands to the eternal credit of the comrades of Wallace that they do not appear – not one of them – to have taken a single step to better or shield themselves by ignominious treachery to their undaunted friend.

Apparently Wallace and Fraser had got together some followers again after their defeat at Peebles and had drawn towards Stirling in the hope of effecting some diversion in favour of the gallant garrison. They do not, however, seem to have been strong enough to contribute any useful support. After the capitulation of Stirling Castle, an English force appears to have proceeded against them, for in September there is record of a pursuit after Wallace 'under Earnside'. But there are no particulars available: the record affords but a momentary glimpse into the darkness.

Meantime the attempt to capture Wallace was steadily kept up by Edward and his emissaries. On 28 February 1305, Ralph de Haliburton, who was, unhappily for his honour, one of the Scots survivors of the siege of Stirling Castle, was released from prison in England and delivered to Sir John de Mowbray, 'of Scotland, knight,' to be taken to Scotland 'to help those Scots that were seeking to capture Sir William Wallace.' It stands on record that Sir John and others gave security to re-enter Ralph at the parliament in London in three weeks from Easter (18 April), 'after seeing what he can do.' But, so far as appears, the miserable renegade was not able to do anything effective. Is this possibly 'Ralph Raa'?

Somewhere about this period may probably be placed an episode in the chequered career of a Scots squire, Michael de Miggel, who had been in Wallace's hands if not actually of his company. Michael had done homage to Edward in the crowd on 14 March 1296 but had promptly repented, for in six weeks' time he was taken prisoner in Dunbar Castle. For eighteen months thereafter he was confined in the Castle of Nottingham, which may probably indicate that the English officers were aware that he needed to be strictly looked after. On 1 September 1305, an inquisition was held at Perth 'on certain articles touching the person of Michael de Miggel', the substantial charge apparently being that he had been a confederate of Wallace. The sworn statement of the inquisitors was 'that he had been lately taken prisoner forcibly against his will by William le Waleys; that he escaped once from William for two leagues, but was followed and brought back by some armed accomplices of William's, who was firmly resolved to kill him for his flight; that he escaped another time from said William for three leagues or more, and was again brought back a prisoner by force with the greatest violence, and hardly avoided death at William's hands, had not some accomplices of William's spoke up for him; whereupon he was told if he tried to get away a third time he should lose his life. Thus it appears,' they concluded, 'he remained with William through fear of death, and not of his own will.' The explanation served. The date 'lately' in all probability places the episode in the last few months of Wallace's career. It at least confirms the strenuous persistence of Wallace, as far as his means would permit, against the enemies of his country and their relentless hunting down of all his adherents.

Unable to maintain himself in the east, Wallace retired to the west. Whether Harry is right or wrong in making Sir Aymer de Valence bargain with Sir John de Menteith for the capture of the patriot matters little; the result is the same. Menteith, in any case, took up the hunt. It has been said that he was then Edward's man. True, he was Edward's man, and since 20 March 1304 he had been Constable of Dumbarton Castle and town and Sheriff of Dumbartonshire. He was therefore acting in the plain way of duty. At the same time, the previous question remains to be disposed of: why was he, a Scots knight, the man of the English king? Instead of lessening the severity of his infamy, his official position only deepens its blackness. Harry finds a much more plausible excuse for the poor-spirited creature. Harry depicts him as displaying reluctance, as urging to Sir Aymer:

> 'He is our governor;
> For us he stood in many a felon stour,
> Not for himself, but for our heritage:
> To sell him thus it were a foul outrage.'

Harry appears to think that Menteith was Constable of Dumbarton in Wallace's interest, and the dramatic remonstrance he puts into Menteith's mouth is sufficiently transparent. However, it elicits from Sir Aymer a promise that Wallace's life shall be safe and that Edward will be satisfied if his great enemy is securely lodged in prison. On this promise, Menteith consents. True or untrue, it is the only decent plea that has ever been suggested on Menteith's behalf, and even then it disgraces his intelligence. Harry further indicates that Menteith, after all, delayed somewhat in the execution of the project. He says that Edward wrote to Menteith privately and 'prayed him to haste'.

Menteith proceeded to carry out his scheme. Harry says he got 'his sister's son' to attach himself to Wallace's personal following with full instructions for the betrayal. The youth was to inform Menteith of Wallace's movements so as to enable him to effect the capture under the most favourable conditions. This subordinate tool is said to have been named Jack Short. Tthe authority of Langtoft is usually given, but mistakenly. It is not Langtoft, but Langtoft 'illustrated and improved' by Robert of Brunne, that mentions 'Jack Short his man' as the instrument of Wallace's betrayal, adding by way of explanation that 'Jack's brother had he slain.'

The desired opportunity soon offered itself. According to Harry, Bruce, in reply to an invitation to come and claim the crown, informed Wallace that he would devise an excuse for leaving the English court and endeavour to meet him on Glasgow Moor on the first night of July. Attended only by the ever faithful Kerly and the treacherous emissary of Menteith, Wallace rode out on several evenings from Glasgow to Robroyston in expectation of Bruce. On 'the eighth night', Menteith received notice, and with sixty sworn men – 'of his own kin, and of kinsmen born' – he hurried to the scene. About midnight, Wallace and Kerly went to sleep – a very unlikely thing for Kerly to do in the circumstances. The traitorous attendant then is said to have removed their arms and given the signal to Menteith. Kerly was instantly dispatched. Wallace started up and, missing his arms, defended himself with his hands. Menteith then came forward and declared that resistance was in vain, the house being surrounded by English troops, that the English really did not wish to kill him and that he would be safe under his protection in his own house in Dumbarton Castle. Wallace thought that Menteith, 'his gossip twice' (for Major, in agreement with Harry, records that Wallace had stood godfather to two of Menteith's children), might be trusted; still he made him swear. As Harry remarks, 'That wanted wit; what should his oaths avail any more, seeing he had been long forsworn to him?' The oath taken, Wallace resigned his hands to the 'sure cords' of Menteith.

As they fared forth, Wallace saw no Southrons, and he missed Kerly – to him convincing signs of betrayal. Still Menteith protested that the sole intention was to keep their prisoner in security; there was no design against his life. The

167

truth, however, was at once evident. Menteith did not proceed to Dumbarton but took his way south with all speed, 'aye holding the waste land', for 'the traitors durst not pass where Scotsmen were masters', and it was essential to their purpose to gain time on Wallace's men and to confuse the certain pursuit. On the south side of 'Solway sands', Menteith delivered Wallace to Sir Aymer de Valence and Sir Robert de Clifford, who conducted him 'full fast' to Carlisle where they threw him into prison. His real custodian, however, appears to have been Sir John de Segrave, the Warden south of Forth.

Such writers as exculpate Menteith from participation in the capture of Wallace must explain the following facts. There still exists a document that looks like a memorandum of business for Edward's parliament or council. It notes that 40 marks are to be given to the vallet who spied out William Wallace; that 60 marks are to be given to the others and that the king desires they shall divide the money among them; and that £100 in land is to be given to John de Menteith. Again, shortly after the middle of September, when the Scots commissioners attended the English parliament for the special purpose of agreeing to regulations for the settlement of Scotland, nine, instead of ten, appeared, and in place of Earl Patrick, who was the absent member, Sir John de Menteith 'by the King's command was chosen.' By one of the regulations then agreed to, Sir John de Menteith was confirmed in the governorship of Dumbarton Castle. Further, on 20 November 1305, a signal mark of royal favour is recorded with peculiar emphasis. At the request of 'his faithful and loyal John de Menteith,' Edward commands his Chancellor to issue letters of protection and safe-conduct in favour of certain burgesses of St Omer passing with their goods and merchandise through his dominions, the letters to be framed in such especial form as John de Menteith shall wish 'in reason', to last for two or three years as pleases him most. The Chancellor is to deliver them without delay to Menteith and to no other, for the king has granted them to him 'with much regret', and would have given them to no other than himself. And finally, on 16 June 1306, Edward commands Sir Aymer de Valence to deliver to Sir John de Menteith the temporality of the bishopric of Glasgow towards Dumbarton, during pleasure, and on the same date he informs Sir Aymer that he has ordered the Chancellor and Chamberlain to prepare a charter granting the Earldom of the Lennox to Sir John de Menteith, 'as one to whom he is much beholden for his good service, as Sir Aymer tells him, and he hears from others,' and he commands Sir Aymer to give him seisin (feudal possession of land). Harry may have mixed up the facts a little, but it is plain that he has got hold of the main thread. Apart from the capture of Wallace, it is simply incredible that Menteith's services would have been deemed so markedly valuable in the eyes of the English king.

Having told Edward of the capture of his great enemy, Valence and Clifford brought Wallace on to London. Harry says Valence and Clifford, but no doubt he ought to have said Sir John de Segrave; at any rate, Wallace was in the custody of Segrave on 18 August. The news of Wallace's coming had spread far and wide, and as the cavalcade approached the capital, it was met by a multitude of men and women, curious to gaze upon the rebellious savage – says Stow, 'wondering upon him.' The illustrious captive was lodged in the house of Alderman William de Leyre, in the parish of All-hallows Staining, at the end of Fenchurch Street. It may seem strange that he was not taken to the Tower. In any case, it is in the last degree improbable that the fact points to any intention of Edward to make a final attempt to secure Wallace's submission to his grace. There is certainly more probability in Carrick's conjecture that the reason was 'the difficulty which the party encountered in making their way through the dense multitudes who blocked up the streets and lanes leading to the Tower'. The date of the arrival was Sunday 22 August.

No time was lost. Everything was in readiness. The very next morning, Monday 23 August 1305, Wallace was conducted on horseback from the City to Westminster to undergo the farce of trial. Sir John de Segrave was in command of the escort, and with him there rode the mayor, sheriffs, and aldermen of London, followed by a great number of people on horseback and on foot. When he arrived at Westminster Hall, Wallace was placed on a bench on the south side. It is said that as he sat there awaiting his doom, he was crowned with a garland of laurel leaves. The popular English fancy absurdly associated this strange procedure with an alleged assertion of Wallace's in times past, to the effect that he deserved to wear a crown in that Hall. Some writers regard it as a mark of derision. Llewelyn's head had been exposed on the battlements of the Tower crowned with a wreath of ivy – said to be in fulfilment of a prophecy of Merlin's. Sir Simon Fraser is said, in the ballad, to have been drawn through the streets to the gallows with 'a garland on his head after the new guise', although Langtoft says Fraser's head was fixed on London Bridge 'without chaplet of flowers', as if the omission were a noticeable breach of custom. It is a mistake, then, to suppose that the garland was a special insult to Wallace. It may have marked the satisfaction of victory over a notable enemy.

The Commissioners appointed to try Wallace were Sir John de Segrave, Sir Peter Malory, the Lord Chief Justice, Ralph de Sandwich, the Constable of the Tower, John de Bacwell (or Banquelle), a judge, and Sir John le Blound (Blunt), Mayor of London. They had been appointed by Edward on 18 August. They were all present. The indictment was comprehensive, charging sedition, homicide, spoliation and robbery, arson and various other felonies. The charge of sedition or treason was based on Edward's conquest of Scotland. On Balliol's forfeiture, he had reduced all the Scots to his lordship and royal power, had publicly received homage and fealty from the prelates, earls, barons and a multitude of others, had proclaimed his peace throughout Scotland, and had appointed wardens, his lieutenants, sheriffs and others, officers and men, to maintain his peace and to do justice. Yet this Wallace, forgetful of his fealty and allegiance, had risen against his lord, had banded together a great number of felons and feloniously attacked the king's wardens and men, had, in particular, attacked, wounded and slain William de Hazelrig, Sheriff of Lanark, and, in contempt of the king, had cut the said Sheriff's body in pieces, had assailed towns, cities and castles of Scotland, had made his writs run throughout the land as if he were Lord Superior of that realm, and, having driven out of Scotland all the wardens and servants of the Lord King, had set up and held parliaments and councils of his own. More than that, he had counselled the prelates, earls and barons, his adherents, to submit themselves to the fealty and lordship of the king of France, and to aid that sovereign to destroy the realm of England. Further, he had invaded the realm of England, entering the counties of Northumberland, Cumberland and Westmoreland, and committing horrible enormities. He had feloniously slain all he had found in these places, liegemen of the king. He had not spared any person that spoke the English tongue but put to death, with all the severities he could devise, all – old men and young, wives and widows, children and sucklings. He had slain the priests and the nuns, and burned down the churches, 'together with the bodies of the saints and other relics of them therein placed in honour.' In such ways, day by day and hour by hour, he had seditiously and feloniously persevered, to the danger alike of the life and the crown of the Lord King. For all that, when the Lord King invaded Scotland with his great army and defeated William, who opposed him in a pitched battle, and others his enemies, and granted his firm peace to all of that land, he had mercifully had the said William Wallace recalled to his peace. Yet William, persevering seditiously and feloniously in his wickedness, had rejected his overtures with indignant scorn and refused to submit himself to the king's peace. Therefore, in the court of the Lord King, he had been publicly outlawed, according to the laws and customs of England and Scotland, as a misleader of the lieges, a robber and a felon.

It was laid down as not consonant with the laws of England that a man so placed beyond the pale of the laws and not afterwards restored to the king's peace should be admitted either to defend himself or to plead. Still it is recorded that Wallace, whether regularly or irregularly, did reply to Sir Peter Malory, denying that he had ever been a traitor to the

English king. He is also said to have acknowledged the other charges preferred. There are allegations of wanton and extravagant misdeeds that undoubtedly merited denial and could not have been positively acknowledged by Wallace. It may be that he considered it futile to raise any further objection and heard the charges with the contempt of silent indifference.

Sentence was pronounced:

'That the said William, for the manifest sedition that he practised against the Lord King himself, by feloniously contriving and acting with a view to his death and to the abasement and subversion of his crown and royal dignity, by opposing his liege lord in war to the death, be drawn from the Palace of Westminster to the Tower of London, and from the Tower to Aldgate, and so through the midst of the City, to the Elms;

'And that for the robberies, homicides, and felonies he committed in the realm of England and in the land of Scotland, he be there hanged, and afterwards taken down from the gallows;

'And that, inasmuch as he was an outlaw, and was not afterwards restored to the peace of the Lord King, he be decollated and decapitated;

'And that thereafter, for the measureless turpitude of his deeds towards God and Holy Church in burning down churches, with the vessels and litters wherein and whereon the body of Christ and the bodies of saints and relics of these were placed, the heart, the liver, the lungs, and all the internal organs of William's body, whence such perverted thoughts proceeded, be cast into fire and burnt;

'And further, that inasmuch as it was not only against the Lord King himself, but against the whole Community of England and of Scotland, that he committed the aforesaid acts of sedition, spoliation, arson, and homicide, the body of the said William be cut up and divided into four parts; and that the head, so cut off, be set up on London Bndge, in the sight of such as pass by, whether by land or by water; and that one quarter be hung on a gibbet at Newcastle-upon-Tyne, another quarter at Berwick, a third quarter at Stirling, and the fourth at St Johnston, as a warning and a deterrent to all that pass by and behold them.'

In execution of this atrocious sentence, Wallace was dragged at the tails of horses through the streets of London to the Elms in Smithfield (i.e. Smoothfield – later Cow Lane, then King Street). At the foot of the gallows, he is said to have asked for a priest in order to make confession. Harry seems confused in placing this incident before the procession to Westminster, and his representation of the Archbishop of Canterbury as shriving Wallace in defiance of Edward's express general prohibition is at any rate highly coloured in the details. Harry further records that Wallace requested Clifford to let him have the psalter that he habitually carried with him and that, when this was brought, Wallace got a priest to hold it open before him 'till they to him had done all that they would.' The head was fixed on London Bridge, and the four quarters were taken to their destined places of exposure by Segrave. The chroniclers vary in the names of these places, Dumfries and Aberdeen being specified by one or another instead of towns mentioned above. There still exists an account presented by the Sheriffs of London on 1 December for:

'15 shillings. delivered to John de Segrave in August last for carriage of the body of William le Waleys to Scotland, by the Kings writ; and John's receipt.'

174

The record adds that 'afterwards they were allowed 10 shillings. in the Roll' – a last royal meanness in connection with Wallace.

Wallace was dead. Laboriously tracked and hunted down by miserable hirelings – Scots, to their black shame – he had been put through the farce of a formal trial and done to death by an accumulation of barbarous cruelties and indignities. Wallace had never done homage or sworn fealty to the English king: how could he possibly be a traitor? His deadly crime, in fact, was that he alone of all the prominent Scotsmen of the time had never bowed to the usurper. Many a real traitor – doubly, trebly and deeper dyed – had Edward let off with little or no punishment and even restored to their estates and to his own favour and confidence. But let a man show the genuine mettle of an independent spirit and his fate was sealed. Wallace could not be bent; therefore he must be broken. In loose popular language he might be called a traitor, and the justices of the special Commission were not inclined to split technical hairs of legality. But in fact Wallace was simply a prisoner of war, an open enemy captured in arms. Under judicial forms he was doomed to death in accordance with a prearranged programme under which there was no necessity for the prosecution to call evidence and no opportunity for the victim to offer any defence. Of course his life was justly at the king's mercy. But Wallace died, not because his life was technically forfeited but simply because Edward could feel no security so long as his arch-enemy breathed. The formality of trial was a mere abuse of judicial process, calculated to fool people already disposed to be fooled. Once more Edward took care to shelter himself under the forms of legal procedure.

The elaborate series of punishments assigned to the various categories of Wallace's alleged misdeeds illustrates forcibly the vindictiveness of Edward. A soldier like him might have been expected to show soldierly appreciation of the most gallant enemy he ever faced. The zeal manifested in vengeance for the alleged dishonour to God and the holy saints is sufficiently edifying, even for the early years of the fourteenth century. It cloaks the malignant gratification of personal malice with the dazzling profession of the championship of religion. When the spacious Abbey of Dunfermline was burnt to the ground only eighteen months before, that was presumably not for the dishonour, but for the glory, of God and the holy saints. The point of view is notoriously important.

Wallace was dead. his body was dismembered and distributed in the great centres of his activity and influence as an encouragement to English sympathizers and a sign of retribution to Scots that might yet cherish the foolishness of patriotism. The moral has been well rendered by Burton:

'The death of Wallace stands forth among the violent ends which have had a memorable place in history. Proverbially such acts belong to a policy that outwits itself. but the retribution has seldom come so quickly, and so utterly in defiance of all human preparation and calculation, as here. Of the bloody trophies sent to frighten a broken people into abject subjection, the bones had not yet been bared ere they became tokens to deepen the wrath and strengthen the courage of a people arising to try the strength of the bands by which they were bound, and, if possible, break them once and for ever.'

Wallace had done his work right well and truly, as builder of the foundations of Scottish independence. He had sealed his faith with his blood. Probably he died despairing of his country. Yet barely had six months come and gone when his dearest wish was fulfilled. The banner of freedom waved defiance from the towers of Lochmaben, and in the Chapel Royal of Scone the Bruce was crowned king of Scotland.

CHAPTER IX

THE PATRIOT HERO

'Lawta and trowth was ay in Wallace seyn;
To fend the rycht all that he tuk on hand.'
                                        Harry, viii, 144–5
'The manlyast man, the starkest off persoun,
Leyffand he was; and als stud in sic rycht
We traist weill God his dedis had in sycht.'
                                        Harry, ix, 616–18

It is matter of deep regret that the facts of the personality
and career of Wallace still remain so obscure. There is no alternative but to piece them together painfully from the
strange miscellany of available materials, perplexed, dis-
torted, fragmentary and fabulous. Yet when the misrepresen-
tations of virulent foes and adulatory admirers are firmly
brushed away, the patriot hero stands forth, incontestably, as
one of the grandest figures of history.

On the death of Alexander III, Scotland sank from the
crest of prosperity into the very trough of adversity. The
brief reigns of the infant Margaret and the puppet Balliol
served only as breathing space for the marshalling of the
forces of internal conflict to the profit of a powerful and remorseless aggressor. Industry was unsettled; commerce was

disorganized. The king was treated with contempt; the nobles were distrusted. Both king and nobles were liegemen of the foreigner, while the free commons sullenly nourished the passion of immemorial independence. Scotland was indeed 'stad in perplexytè'. Her 'gold wes changyd in to lede'. When and whence would ever come succour and remede?

Succour and remede sprang, naturally, from the insolence and oppression of the minions of the invader. Little did Wallace know of the solemn farce enacted at Norham and Berwick or of the feudal rights of Balliol or another. Like a deliverer of old, 'he went out unto his brethren, and looked on their burdens.' 'When he saw there was no man, he slew the Englishman, and hid him in the sand.' An outlaw, he drew to him friends, free lances, probably enough desperadoes, and waged such guerrilla warfare as was possible against the oppressors of his family and his countrymen. Some other knights and squires similarly maintained themselves in the forests and fastnesses of the land. But there must have been some distinctive and commanding qualities in the man who was able to step forward in that dark hour from an obscure social position to lead the forlorn hope of Scottish independence.

'Wallace's make, as he grew up to manhood,' says Tytler, 'approached almost to the gigantic; and his personal strength was superior to the common run of even the strongest men.' Even Burton dissociates himself from belief in this statement. But surely, although 'the later romancers and minstrels' have 'profusely trumpeted Wallace's personal prowess and superhuman strength', the assertion of Tytler makes no great demand on one's credulity. On the contrary, in an age when warlike renown depended so essentially on personal deeds of derring-do, the astonishing thing – the incredible thing – would be if Wallace had not been a man of pre-eminent physical strength and resourcefulness in the use of arms. By what other means, indeed, could the second son of an obscure knight, a mere youth just out of his teens, living the life of an outlaw, uncountenanced by the support of a single great noble, by any possibility have maintained himself, attracted adherents, impressed the enemy and become the hero of a nation, if he did not possess quite exceptional physical strength and prowess? How is it possible that a man who had gone through the hardships of a desperate guerrilla campaign, as Wallace must have done, should be other than a man 'of iron frame'? Ajax was taller than Agamemnon, and Jop may have stood a head higher than Wallace. But the substantial fact of his impressive physique is not to be denied. The romancers exaggerate, of course, but on this point even Harry scarcely outdoes Major or Bower.

Harry's slight sketch of Wallace as a 'child' of eighteen prepares us for the description of his hero in his prime by 'clerks, knights, and heralds' of France, which, he says, Blair set down 'in Wallace' book'.

> 'Wallace' stature, in largeness and in height,
> Was judged thus, by such as saw him right
> Both in his armour dight and in undress:
> Nine quarters large he was in length – no less;
> Third part his length in shoulders broad was he,
> Right seemly, strong, and handsome for to see;
> His limbs were great, with stalwart pace and sound;
> His brows were hard, his arms were great and round;
> His hands right like a palmer's did appear,
> Of manly make, with nails both great and clear;

Proportioned long and fair was his visage;
Right grave of speech, and able in courage;
Broad breast and high, with sturdy neck and great,
Lips round, his nose square and proportionate;
Brown wavy hair, on brows and eyebrows light,
Eyes clear and piercing, like to diamonds bright.
On the left side was seen below the chin,
By hurt, a wen; his colour was sanguine.
Wounds, too, he had in many a diverse place,
But fair and well preserved was aye his face.
Of riches for himself he kept no thing;
Gave as he won, like Alexander the King.
In time of peace, meek as a maid was he;
Where war approached, the right Hector was he.
To Scots men ever credence great he gave;
Known enemies could never him deceive.
These qualities of his were known in France,
Where people held him in good remembrance.'

It is futile to dispute fractional details. Let the most exacting historical critic array the indisputable facts of Wallace's birth, breeding and career, and frame upon these his conception of the figure of the man. It is impossible that there should be any substantial difference between such a picture and the picture exhibited by Harry. Fordun states that Wallace was 'wondrously brave and bold, of goodly mien, and boundless liberality'; and that he ruled with an iron hand of discipline. Major declines to commit himself to Wallace's alleged feats of strength, yet he does not scruple to affirm that 'two or even three Englishmen were scarce able to make stand against him, such was his bodily strength, such also the quickness of his dexterity, and his indomitable courage,' while 'there was no extreme of cold or heat, or hunger or of thirst, that he could not bear.' And Bower's description bears out fully the account given by Harry. The objector is not to be envied in his task of explaining how Wallace fought in the thickest of the battle, how he defended the rear against mailed horsemen on barbed chargers, and how he stood at the head of the Scots in the battle of Stirling Bridge

But, as Burton justly remarks, 'Wallace's achievements demanded qualities of a higher order.' Now Burton's cautious reticence gives especial emphasis to his decided affirmation that Wallace 'was a man of vast political and military genius.' 'As a soldier,' the circumspect Burton freely admits, 'Wallace was one of those marvellously gifted men, arising at long intervals, who can see through the military superstitions of the day, and organize power out of those elements which the pedantic soldier rejects as rubbish.'

Yes, Wallace had to create, and then to train, not merely to organize and marshal and order in the field. Wallace started with the sole equipment of his single sword. With his small and inexperienced body of comrades, without mailed barons or mailed chargers, he was driven by sheer necessity to devise means of conserving his force and at the same time making it as effective as possible in offence. At Stirling, his masterly selection of the ground practically decided the issue; the rash confidence of Cressingham only rendered the victory more complete. At Falkirk, as Burton points out, 'he showed even more of the tactician in the disposal of his troops where they were compelled to fight' – tactics amply vindicated on many a modern battlefield. 'The arrangement, save that it was circular instead of rectangular, was precisely the same as the 'square to receive cavalry' which has baffled and beaten back so many a brilliant army in later days.' But for the defection of the cavalry, comparatively weak as they were, Falkirk might have been Stirling Bridge. These tactics, however, admirable as they are universally acknowledged to have been, and even original, were no doubt developed by painful experience in the guerrilla period. And, on the other hand, it is to be remembered that while Scotland had had no experience of war for more than a century, Wallace was not only crippled by the operation of the feudal allegiance but had for his opponents the ablest generals and the most seasoned warriors of the age.

On the moral side of war, Wallace must indeed have been a barbarian if any apology for his severities is due to the murderers of his wife, to the conqueror who made Berwick swim in blood, to the insolent tramplers upon the common human feelings of his countrymen or to the juggling reivers of the independence of his country. We decline to apologize for his alleged private reprisals: if you madden a man with open injustice and intolerable oppression, if you lacerate his soul in his physical helplessness, it is you yourself who invite him to have recourse to the primal code of retaliation. If Wallace, as Harry says, never spared any Englishman 'that able was to war', it was an intelligible principle in the dire circumstances of the time; and he is not known to have deprecated the application of the principle to himself. If he imagined that there had come to him an admonition, divine and imperative, to slay and spare not, we decline to censure him because he hewed his enemies in pieces before the Lord.

Yet such deliberate and inexorable rigour of policy is a wholly different matter from gratuitous cruelty. Wallace did

183

not war on women, priests or other 'weak folk'. It is not the strong man who is a cruel man. True, the English historians brand him as brigand, cut-throat, man of Belial, and so forth – *latro ille, latro publicus*, etc – and ascribe to him inhuman atrocities. This indeed is by no means unnatural for writers of the cloister, starting from Wallace's outlawry and his guerrilla warfare, and cherishing a full share of the virulent international enmity. But while no doubt very rough deeds were done in those days on both sides, 'Herodian cruelties' are merely the stock allegations of dislike at this period and they are hurled from both sides indiscriminately. Major expressly admits that 'towards all unwarlike persons, such as women and children, towards all who claimed his mercy, he showed himself humane,' although 'the proud and all who offered resistance he knew well how to curb.' The strong impression remains that Wallace never, at any rate never without some overpowering constraint, either did or permitted mere cruelty to any person. Hemingburgh's account of the episode at Hexham speaks volumes in his favour.

The regrettable inadequacy of historical criticism of Harry's poem prevents us, in the meantime, from illustrating the minor military qualities of Wallace. But, admitted that he was 'a man of vast military genius', there is little necessity for detailed remarks on his care and consideration for his men, on his men's confidence in him and affection for him, on his sleepless vigilance, his high courage, his cool daring, his masterful rule, his resolute tenacity and endurance, his keen sense of honour, his singular unselfishness, his lofty magnanimity. Undoubtedly he did not lack that 'bit of the devil in him,' without which, according to Sir Charles Napier, 'no man can command.' Nothing in all Harry's panorama is more nobly touching, or more illustrative than the faithfulness of the men who stood closest to Wallace. Is it not true, although Harry says it, that, when Steven of Ireland and Kerly rejoined their lost leader in the Tor Wood after the annihilation of Elcho Park, 'for perfect joy they wept with all their een'? Is not the lament of Wallace over the dead body of Sir John the Graham on the field of Falkirk the true, as well as the supreme, expression of the profound affection and confidence that united the goodly fellowship of these tried comrades and dauntless men?

Burton, as we have seen, also acknowledges freely that Wallace was 'a man of vast political genius'. The particulars are most limited and yet they are ample to ground a large inference. It will be sufficient to recall his endeavours in the midst of warlike activity to resuscitate industry and commerce, to reorganize the civil order, to secure the aid of France and Rome, to minimize the friction with the barons and to observe and to enforce deference to constitutional principle. It is a striking testimony to his greatness of mind that he was absolutely destitute of ambition as ambition is ordinarily understood. Emphatically he was a man who

'cared not to be great,
But as he saved or served the State.'

Even at the height of his power and popularity, he does not seem to have had the faintest impulse to seize the crown, or indeed to seize anything, for himself. Harry tells an extraordinary story, with a definiteness that commands attention, how he took the crown for one day on Northallerton Moor expressly and solely and most reluctantly 'to get battle.'

185

Whether he could have taken the crown and held it – if he had so wished – need not tempt speculation. It is a singularly bright leaf in Wallace's laurels that there remains no shadow of evidence of any inclination on his part to swerve from the straight course of pure and unselfish patriotism.

'Wallace,' says Major, 'whom the common people, with some of the nobles, followed gladly, had a lofty spirit; and born, as he was, of no illustrious house, he yet proved himself a better ruler in the simple armour of his integrity than any of those nobles would have been.' And again: 'Wise and prudent he was, and marked throughout his life by a loftiness of aim which gives him a place, in my opinion, second to none in his day and generation.'

But beyond and above the exceptional tribute of 'vast political and military genius' – a tribute doubly ample for any one man in any century of a nation's history – it is the unique glory of Wallace that he was the one man of his time who dared to champion the independence of his country More than that, although he died a cruel and shameful death amidst the exultant insults of his country's foes in the capital city of the enemy, he yet died victorious. He had kept alight the torch of Scottish freedom. He, a man of the people, had taught the disloyal nobles that resistance to the invader was not hopeless, although those who took the torch immediately from his hand failed to carry it on; and the light was preserved by the commonalty until the torch was at length grasped by Bruce. Wallace, in fact, had made the ascendency of Bruce possible – a possibility converted into a certainty by the death of Edward I.

Lord Rosebery justly pointed to the attitude of Edward towards him in 1304, as 'the greatest proof of Wallace's eminence and power.' The true Deliverer of Scotland was Sir William Wallace.

The prime consideration is very finely singled out and expressed by Lord Rosebery in the address he delivered at the Stirling Celebration in 1897:

> 'There are junctures in the affairs of men when what is wanted is a Man – not treasures, not fleets, not legions, but a Man – the man of the moment, the man of the occasion, the man of Destiny, whose spirit attracts and unites and inspires, whose capacity is congenial to the crisis, whose powers are equal to the convulsion – the child and the outcome of the storm....We recognize in Wallace one of these men – a man of Fate given to Scotland in the storms of the thirteenth century. It is that fact, the fact of his destiny and his fatefulness, that succeeding generations have instinctively recognized.'

The instinct of the Scottish nation is thoroughly sound. Alhough at one time nourished by Harry's poem, it is rooted in the rock of historical fact. And despite the sneers of the inconsiderate, it was a great imperial influence. Who could assert that the empire suffered from the intense passion of freedom that Scotsmen associate with the name of Wallace? Is it not the obvious fact that the free national feeling by transmutation swells the imperial flame? If it is fundamentally because of Wallace's heroic heart and mind that the national spirit of freedom saved Scotland from union with England on any terms less dignified than the footing of independence, then the results of his noble struggle entitle him to a foremost place among great men. One sovereign at least of England as well as of Scotland acknowledged – and handsomely acknowledged – 'the good and honourable service done of old by William Wallace for the defence of that our kingdom.' Wallace made Scotland great. And to Scotsmen, in all the generations, Freedom will ever be nobly typified in the immortal name of Sir William Wallace.